Religion, Society, and
Utopia in Nineteenth-
Century America

Religion, Society, and Utopia in Nineteenth-Century America

Ira L. Mandelker

The University
of Massachusetts Press
Amherst, 1984

Copyright © 1984 by
The University of Massachusetts Press
All rights reserved
Printed in the United States of America
LC 84-47
ISBN 0-87023-436-6
Library of Congress Cataloging in
Publication Data appear on the
last page of this book

Acknowledgments

Although their names appear seldom, if at all, in this work, I have counted upon Arthur J. Vidich, Stanford M. Lyman, Jeffrey C. Goldfarb, and the late Benjamin Nelson for inspiration, encouragement, and good sociological sense. Their contribution goes well beyond that which can be acknowledged in footnotes. Any errors of omission, commission, or interpretation are mine alone.

This work is dedicated to Kati Bors Mandelker and the rest of my family for their loving support and patience.

Contents

Part I
Religious Utopia and the Tension between Religion and World

1

Introduction

Millennial, revolutionary, and utopian religious experiments have been perennial subjects of historical, psychological, and sociological analysis. American sociology has, for the most part, taken a rather one-sided approach which has reflected its preeminent concerns with structure and organization. The wealth of studies examining the social structure and organization of utopian religious communities only routinely makes the connection between theology, sacred history, values, and prophecy and the creation of community organization and social structure. But most have failed to critically examine the role of the community's theology, utopian vision, and prophecy in the failure of such experiments, or to recognize the ideological and theological barriers to utopian religious growth.

Rosabeth Moss Kanter's study of ninety-one utopian communities founded between 1780 and 1860 suggests the importance of religion in forging the commitment so vital to utopian success, but analyzes the communities' failures in terms of deteriorating structural and organizational commitment mechanisms. Certainly the presence of commitment mechanisms is important to explaining the success of utopian experiments, but Kanter takes only perfunctory notice of ideological dynamics of failure.[1] Even the utopian experiments that were "successful" in Kanter's terms—those that survived for at least twenty-five years—ultimately failed in the sense that they either dissolved or eventually departed from utopian ideals and collective organization. The question left unanswered is how does ideological commitment deteriorate? The internal dynamics of religious prophecy and beliefs may be important here. This is the path of inquiry we will be following.

Karen and G. E. Stephan have also noted the importance of religion in explaining successful utopian experiments, and their study of 143 utopian communes that existed between 1776 and 1900 suggests that "the success of communes, measured in terms of the length of time they survived, seems to depend upon whether or not their ideological foundations included adherence to a single, established religion. Although 'success' was rare in any case, those which did achieve it appear to have been those with a religious orientation."[2] Utopian "failures" enter Stephan and Stephan's analysis only to the extent that they allow us to identify the "successes." Failures are described in terms of a characteristic that is absent, and the dynamics of utopian experiments are beyond the scope of their work.

Harry Hawthorne touches upon our issue briefly.[3] He reminds us that literary and philosophical utopias are "among the duller works of human imagination" due to their static and fixed character and that, although actual utopian experiments are far from dull, their static social and cultural order has led to failure after a relatively short period of time. He wonders whether there is a parallel between the poor literary quality of fictional utopias and the bad social engineering of actual experiments. Where fictional utopian fixity has no consequence beyond literary and philosophical criticism, the failures of actual utopian experiments are related to their inability to cope with deviancy and change in a rationally comprehensive manner. Static utopian communities are doomed to failure because of their intransigence and unwillingness to accept change as inherent to the social order. Success requires separating the moral order from the social order and viewing the latter as subject and susceptible to change without destroying the community. In short, a measure of expediency is required to insure the community's continuity. Hawthorne seems to at least implicitly recognize our issue, but fails to ask the critical question: At what point does dynamism undermine ideals, transforming the utopia from a value-based community to one whose fundamental value is community?

To some extent, Marin Lockwood Carden's study of the Oneida

Community suggests that the internal dynamics of religious belief are significant in explaining the community's decline.[4] The community's founder and charismatic leader, John Humphrey Noyes, went well beyond other nineteenth-century Perfectionists' theological innovations. His hermeneutically derived freedom from law, tradition, and convention propelled a progressivism that encouraged excessive innovation. The dictates of Oneida Perfectionism, claims Carden, were ultimately used by Noyes to justify a subtle turning away from religion toward social reformism. His later work—*The History of American Socialisms* and the last community periodical, the *American Socialist*—reflected this new interest. Constance Noyes Robertson's work on the breakup, however, makes use of recently found letters, diaries, and journals and brings to light new evidence that Noyes *did not* lose personal interest in religion or soft-pedal it to the community in his later years.[5] Although his interests did widen, religion remained his central concern and stood paramount in his advice and correspondence to the community. Without this theological aspect of Carden's study, we are left with an organizational and structural analysis of how a utopian community deteriorated into a secular, ideological community. If an exhaustive study of the sociology of religious utopian movements was our interest, we would have to go well beyond the small critical distillate offered. These studies are merely representative of a predominantly structural approach to understanding the social and cultural dynamics of utopian religious communities. Our concern will shift to the ideological/theological level. Attention to sacred histories and utopian values and prophecy suggests different questions and relationships for analysis: (1) What is the relationship between secular values and worldviews, and the sacred values and worldviews that are the raison d'être for utopian religious experiments? (2) To what extent, if any, does the relationship between sacred and secular values and worldviews reverberate in the social structure of utopian religious experiments? (3) What are the consequences of the relationship between sacred and secular value structures for the growth and stability, the success or failure of utopian religious experiments?

We will use Max Weber's sociology of religion and the Oneida Community, a Perfectionist community that thrived in the "burned-over" district of New York State in the mid-nineteenth century, to explore these questions and expose their practical and theoretical significance.

Max Weber and the Tension between Religion and World

In his essay "Religious Rejections of the World and Their Directions,"[6] Max Weber provides a suggestive theoretical framework for studying the dynamics and interaction of sacred and secular value spheres: the relationship between the values and ideals promulgated by salvation religions, and the values, logics, and goals of the secular domain is one of inherent tension. First, the natural sib has had to fear devaluation in the face of a prophecy of salvation. Once prophecies of salvation have produced religious communities, the emergent ethic of brotherliness implores one to break the bonds of the household and immerse oneself in the wider community of the brethren of faith. The New Testament counsels that those who cannot be hostile to the members of the household, to father and mother, cannot be disciples of Jesus. The true believer, the faithful, must ultimately stand closer to the savior, prophet, or priest than to blood relations.

Similarly, the values of religion and world collide in the economic sphere, where a rational economy oriented toward money, prices, profits, and calculability makes it less accessible to an ethic of brotherliness that insists upon reciprocity and mutual support.

The tension between salvation religion and the political order arose when barriers of tribe, polity, and locality were shattered by universalist religion. The more rational the political order became, the greater was the tension from the demands of brotherliness. Bureaucracy, as a state apparatus discharging its functions according to formal rules and procedures, operates without regard to persons, hence without hate or love. Furthermore, the state's absolute end of maintaining or transforming the distribution of power within and without its borders, and its monopoly over the legitimate use of violence to resolve questions of "right," can only seem meaningless to ethically oriented salvation religions.

Sex and eroticism may directly compete with religious sensations of salvation in that the erotic experience, the fading of the "thou," the loss of "self" and alteration of consciousness at the sexual climax, can be interpreted both symbolically and literally—as we shall see in the case of the Oneida Community—as a sacrament equivalent to the mystic experience.

The self-conscious tension between religion and world is greatest when religion faces the sphere of intellectual knowledge, especially where rational empirical thought has consistently moved toward the disenchantment of the world and its transformation into a causal mechanism. Science directly confronts the ethical postulate that the world is God ordained and somehow meaningfully and ethically oriented. Religion claims to offer an ultimate stand toward the world by virtue of a direct grasp of its meaning. "Meaning" is unlocked through illumination rather than intellect. Every increase of rationalism in empirical science increasingly pushes religion into the realm of the irrational.

Salvation religions, which must exist within the world for economic support and propaganda, must somehow come to terms with these tensions. Puritan asceticism, predestination and the ethic of "vocation," and the various forms of mystical devaluation of the world as a significant arena of religious action have been the most successful means of coping with the tension between religion and world. All other solutions are full of compromises and presuppositions that appear dishonest or unacceptable to the ethic of brotherliness.

Religion must either reject the world or compromise in its claim for the hearts, minds, and energies of its believers when they are confronted with a world that insists upon playing by its own rules. But Weber recognized that a transcendence of these tensions was also possible: "The theoretically constructed ideal types of conflicting 'life orders' are merely intended to show that at certain points, such and such internal conflicts are possible and 'adequate.' They are not intended to show that there is no standpoint from which the conflicts may not be resolved in a higher synthesis."[7]

This resolution through a "higher synthesis" is precisely the task of religious utopian experiments in their attempt to create a heaven on earth. The history of the Oneida Community suggests a possible crucial role for sacred histories in the utopian attempt to transcend the inherent tension between the values of salvation religion and the secular world. Prior studies have focused on the Oneida Community's failure to solve organization problems that undermined leadership and commitment.[8] These organizational failures of the Oneida Community run deeper, to the ideological level, and it is here that this study departs from previous analyses. Certainly we will consider the organizational problems faced by the Oneida Community, but in a different light: these problems were expressions of persistent and ultimately irreconcilable tensions between religion and world characteristic of utopian religious experiments in general, and expressed in the Oneida Community's theology and practice. We are not claiming that the difficulties of religious utopias are merely theological.

We do insist that the ideological undercurrents of the religious leap
into utopia have been overlooked or, at best, superficially explored
by sociologists and historians explaining the fragility of religious
utopias. Although intensive study of a single religious community
has a limited value in developing generalizations applicable to utopian religious communities as a whole, there is theoretical importance in pointing to the mode and consequence of conceptions of history in penetrating social structure, mediating the tension between
religion and the world so crucial for a religious leap into utopia, and
perhaps explaining the inherent weakness and fragility of such utopian experiments.

Religious Organization and the Relationship between Ideal and Material Interests

In his analysis of Weber's discussion of church, sect, and mysticism,
Benjamin Nelson uncovers the "circulatory processes" that operate
among church, sect, society, and culture and account for the central
patterns of religious organization.[9] These emerging patterns are likely to be very different depending upon the character of the mix of
"religion" and "world." The most critical determinant of this "circulatory process" is the openings available to church and sect in the
societal and cultural structure. Not only is the dynamic interplay between religion and world central to any conception of the structure
and organization of religious communities, but the specific historical
circumstances—the economy, polity, and cultural milieu within
which a community of the faithful exists—are also crucial in understanding the stagnation, growth, decline, and transformation of religious organization.

Nelson does not reduce the success, stability, and character of religious communities to the consequences of secular forces that either
open or close avenues of development and transformation; in his essay he presents only one side of Weber's coin. We cannot isolate this
approach to the dynamics of religious organizations from the other
thrust of Weber's work—the importance of ideas in explaining action: "Not ideas, but material and ideal interests, directly govern
men's conduct. Yet frequently the 'world images' that have been created by 'ideas' have, like switch-men, determined the tracks along
which action has been pushed by the dynamic of interest."[10]

It is important to use these *two* points of entry in studying the
transformations of religious organizations. Not only must we ex-

plore the wider cultural milieu, but also the structure and content of the religious organizations' core ideas, their prophecy, in order to understand their histories. The tension and mix of religion and world provides the fulcrum that pivots in both directions. Moreover, the sacred history to which a religious community is committed is central in gauging the tension between, and mix of, religion and world.

A sacred history not only provides an orientation toward salvation but also places the secular world in that scheme. Ernest Lee Tuveson has shown sacred histories and their transformations have always had an eye toward either placing or explaining contemporary views of the world in stagnation, progress, decline, or cyclical oscillation within the eschatology in vogue.[11] As such notions of history have embraced both sacred and secular realms, the specific nature of its prophecy may open or close doors of development.

Sacred histories, considered as "utopias" in Mannheim's sense, might indeed "transcend" the tension between religion and world in terms of a "higher synthesis," but Weber, who always shied away from general unqualified theoretical statements, did not examine such attempts that would have revealed the theoretical and practical power of his original insight: the persistent tension between religion and world.

Reformulations of the relation between values of religion and world, perhaps even their dissolution in a "higher synthesis," may only provide a temporary ideational solution. Such a resolution does not seem possible except on the theoretical level. Unless the sacred community of brothers wishes to abruptly sever the ties with the wider community of others through monasticism and complete cultural, social, and economic self-sufficiency, the world still remains a source of potential tension and an alternative arena for action, even if devalued. Fictional and philosophical utopianists can establish inviolable borders separating the utopian from the nonutopian world, but this literary license is unavailable to real-life utopian experiments. The boundary between religion and world, no matter how modified, remains as fertile soil for the renewed growth of tension between these values spheres.

Before proceeding further we should establish precisely what we mean by "tension" between religion and the world. Weber says the following in this regard:

We have taken for granted and presupposed that a large and, for the historical development, an especially important fraction of all cases of prophetic and redemptory religions have lived not only in an acute but in a permanent state of tension in relation to the world and its orders. . . . The more the religions have been true religions of salvation, the greater has this tension been. This follows from the meaning of salvation and from the substance of the prophetic teachings as soon as these develop into an ethic. . . . the further the rationalization and sublimation of the external and internal possession of— in the widest sense—"things worldly" has progressed, the stronger has the tension on the part of religion become. For the rationalization and the conscious sublimation of man's relations to the various spheres of value, external, and internal, as well as religious and secular, have . . . pressed toward making conscious the *internal and lawful autonomy* of the individual spheres; thereby letting them drift into those tensions which remain hidden to the originally naive relation with the external world. This results quite generally from the development of inner- and other-worldly values toward rationality, toward conscious endeavor, and toward sublimation by *knowledge*.[12]

Once processes of rationalization have fragmented unified images of the world—i.e., once the economy, polity, religion, and social relations in general come to take over their own value and logic—secular values become alternative loci for both thought and action. As differentiated spheres of value, the sacred and secular make competing claims on the thoughts, commitments, energies, and activities of individuals and groups. In spite of competing value orientations between religion and world, there is no reason to assume that such tensions as may be created between them must be resolved or smoothed over. It can be argued that contradictory, fragmented, pigeonholings of values to particular social contexts is not only possible but is a fact of modern life, reflecting differentiation in social structure, the relative autonomy of economy, polity, and religion, and our multiple group affiliations.[13]

We will use Weber's theory in our historical analysis of the social and religious context from which the Oneida Community sprang; in our examination of the community's utopian ideas, practice, success, and failure; and in our discussion of the prospects for a lasting transcendence of the tensions between religion and world in religious utopias. To understand the success and failure of the Oneida Community, in terms of its internally generated tensions, we must first consider the thought of John Humphrey Noyes, the founder and spiritual leader of the community.

*The New Sacred History: Postmillennial Progressivism
and the Unification of Religion and World*

Careful reading of the Gospel revealed to John Humphrey Noyes
that Christ gave six predictions regarding his second return: (1) it
would occur immediately after the judgment of the Jews, (2) following fearful signs such as wars, earthquakes, and eclipses, (3) before
the contemporary generation passed away, and (4) before the disciples' ministry to the Jews would be complete. (5) Some who stood
with Jesus would witness the event and (6) his disciple John would
tarry till his coming. With the destruction of the temple at Jerusalem
at the hands of the Romans in A.D. 70, which Noyes interpreted as
the Jews' "judgment," the prophecy was complete.[14].

Those who expected spectacles and miracles at the Second Coming were sorely disappointed. It was an event in the spiritual, not the
natural world. It was to be secret, it came "like a thief in the night,"
viewed by a few select disciples. The outward show—wars, earthquakes, and the temple's destruction—paled against the principal
manifestation in the invisible world. With the Second Coming the
apostolic church—for Noyes the true spiritual nucleus of Christianity—passed into the spiritual world. Rather than being more advanced, the successor church was spiritually immature. The Second
Coming was not the final judgment, only the judgment of the Jews.
The judgment of the Gentiles, the final judgment, lay in the future.
Noyes had broken the historical and spiritual continuity of Christianity and thereby invalidated all claims to ecclesiastical authority
based on historic continuity with the apostles. The only true Christian credential would be present community with Christ.

The radical claim that the Second Coming of Christ was a historical event of the definite past rather than a prophetic forecast for the
future required a new scheme of historical and spiritual development. The era from Adam to Moses, Noyes asserted, was one of sen-
suality and longevity, dominated by the physical faculties of mankind. The second era, from Moses to Christ, was a period of moral
development under the stricture of Mosaic law. Intellectual development, distinguished by the advance of scientific knowledge, characterized the period between Christ and Noyes. Since the spiritual continuity with the primitive Church had been broken, the present was
an era of limited moral and spiritual development. Humanity was
now embarking upon a new period of rapid spiritual growth that
would culminate in its complete regeneration. This era had begun

with the recognition of the true nature of the Second Coming. [15] Man was not living in an age of promise: he was living in the age when prophecy would be fulfilled. In the period between the first and second comings of Christ was to be found the results of a completed religious era. The culmination of the Jewish epoch was nothing less than the entire salvation from sin and perfect holiness in this life. [16]

Noyes felt the orthodox church's historical-spiritual scheme was static, committed to the idea that religious privilege and belief had remained on the same general level since Moses. The new sacred history was dynamic. Each era marks the progressive spiritual and/or intellectual elevation of humanity and culminates in definitive accomplishments. God's plan was progressive but not automatic. Transcendental history was not a frictionless machine that, once set in motion, would continue unabated by virtue of its initial force. Although earthly perfection had been possible since the Second Coming in A.D. 70, it remained unachieved. Prayer, study, and patient waiting on God were necessary but insufficient for personal salvation and perfection. Activism and personal asceticism were required to transform the individual, and perfect men and women would create perfect institutions and transform the world. Like Paul, the ideal man should "keep his face toward God and yet be full of outward activity." [17]

The popular theory, locating the Second Coming in the indefinite future, showed no completed results in individuals or society. All is transition and uncertainty; there is no assured prospect for change in the future. This approach, Noyes asserted, debased the work of Christ. His new sacred history testified to Christ's success and the completion of his mission: he "carried a select of humanity, in one generation, straight through to complete resurrection. This fact is worth everything to faith." It was done once, and could be done again. [18]

Reinterpretation of the course of Christian history radically redefined the relationship between religion and the world. The world was not a trial, a testing ground, or a preparation for the soul's afterlife; nor were the orders of heaven and earth separate and distinct. On completion of Christ's mission, the barrier between heaven and earth was broken. Perfect holiness was possible in this world and the new kingdom of heaven on earth could be established by a regenerate humanity under divine guidance. This God-given promise demanded a mystical and ascetic path to salvation, and presented a license for total renovation of social relations and institutions. The relations and social structure of a spiritually immature world were obstacles to the development of perfect man and the kingdom of heaven on earth.

The dialectical relationship between religion and world had been transcended in what Weber would call a "higher synthesis."[19] Inner-worldly mysticism and asceticism were united and expressed an optimistic ethic. Once people have become obsessed with the possession of Christ in their souls, they can assume to be on the correct path. They may stumble or fall on the path to inner-outer perfection, their external behavior may be flawed, but once their hearts are pure they are secure in their direction.

This belief in a historical Second Coming, coupled with the conviction that the Bible was not a revelation to all but required interpretation by the enlightened and inspired, led Noyes to a progressive notion of perfection. Perfection consisted of the spiritual apprehension of Christ's presence in one's soul, made possible through earnest prayer, study, and patient waiting on God. Noyes himself claimed to have undergone a spiritual cleansing and the forsaking of sin on February 20, 1834. Although confession of Christ gave one a spiritual sense of perfection, no guarantees of sinless behavior were offered. Perfection was not a quality of deeds, but of faith.

The apparent contradiction of spiritual perfection and errant behavior was resolved by Noyes's conception of the nature of man. Man had both an inner- and outer-self. Christ's presence within the soul helps the inner-self gain power over the outer-self, but the individuals themselves must work to bring their behavior into accord with their inner perfection by improving their moral and social character, developing their intellectual capabilities, working to realize their potential, and striving for the spirit of love.[20]

As all may choose to become perfect, mankind will draw closer and closer to perfection with the kingdom of heaven progressively and ultimately extending its dominion over the earth.

Noyes created what John M. Janzen has called "dialectical intentions": "problem-solving propositions which confront and destroy the exhausted paradigms of the culture, and come up with new paradigms clothed in tangible, often idiomatic form."[21] The reinterpretation of Scripture and the Second Coming had radically redefined the relationship between religion and world. The tension between religion and world was seemingly dissolved by placing man in the age of fulfillment. In light of this radical reorganization of Christian theology and eschatology, man was given a religious mission: salvation was at hand and could be striven for consciously and conscientiously without the lingering doubt and extreme loneliness experienced by Weber's Puritans. Inner-worldly mysticism and asceticism had been merged theoretically and could be expressed in a relatively optimistic ethic. Once man had become secure in the possession of Christ in his soul, he is assumed to be on the correct path. He may dawdle on the road to inner-outer perfection, but he is on his way nonetheless.

Between 1841 and 1844 Noyes saw the need for the formation of a true community. Only a complete separation from the world would preserve his followers from contradictory doctrine and allow the institution of his Perfectionist ideal. Throughout the literature on Noyes's Putney and Oneida communities, one does not get the impression that he was rejecting the world as such, but that he viewed himself as an explorer charting the seas of salvation beyond the horizon. The social-religious experiment at Oneida was to be the vanguard of the kingdom of heaven on earth in which ultimately all would participate. In May 1846, Noyes initiated among a small circle of early followers a system of "complex marriage" designed to eliminate the fundamental obstacles to universal love—monogamous marriage and "exclusive love"—and to introduce the heavenly form of amative and sexual relations. The Putney Community agreed to absolute communalism including people as well as possessions. Rumors rapidly spread to, and throughout, Putney, Vermont. Noyes attempted to explain and defend his actions and ideas but was forced to leave Putney in November 1847 when he was charged with adultery. A small Perfectionist group was forming at Oneida, New York, and Noyes and his followers—thirty-one adults and four children—were invited to join. At Oneida, Noyes was accepted as the community's sole leader and Christ's representative on earth.

Under Noyes's leadership the community prospered, but as he aged and took a smaller role in the day-to-day management of Oneida's affairs the spiritual consensus that was so important to community commitment deteriorated. By 1881 the "Bible Communists" could find little more than economic interest to keep them together. Many analysts have attributed the decline, failure, and reorganization of the Oneida Community into Oneida Community, Ltd., a joint-stock company professing no religious ideals, to several factors. The declining charisma of its aging and ailing leader, the problems of transferring and routinizing charisma, the attacks of hostile clergy, and intergenerational conflicts are all common themes, but none has focused on the internal theological roots of Oneida's failure. By this I mean the failure to resolve tensions between religion and world once they have arisen *within* the community. The tensions between religion and world generated conflicts over important facets of community life; over sex, marriage, and the family; over economy and political organization; and over religion itself. These conflicts eroded utopian optimism and consensus.

*The Tension between Religion and World in Nineteenth-Century
America and the Oneida Community's Utopian Experiment*

Weber engages the theme of tension between religion and world on the level of the world religions. Our concerns will be much narrower because the grand scale of the world's civilizations might distract us from the idea that these tensions are by no means limited to the theoretical level, but are played out whenever value orientations of religion and world stand face to face. We will search for contradictions, conflicts, and moral and ethical inconveniences that surfaced between religion and world in nineteenth-century American society and culture, and in the smaller utopian domain of the Oneida Community.

The antagonism between religion and economy in New England emerged with the first Puritan settlement. Puritan divines warned their congregations that the harsh struggle to tame the physical environment was deflecting attention and energies from their spiritual duties and concerns. Once the demands of establishing the community lightened and a measure of comfort and prosperity was achieved, the temptation of affluence would try the Puritan soul. But the seeds of conflict between religion and world can be found on a deeper, theological level. Within the Puritan concept of "vocation" we find communal and individualist economic ethics that pulled colonists in opposite directions.

Affluence—generated by a religious ethos that encouraged hard, disciplined work and rational investment—furthered economic individualism and engendered a creeping materialism that was denounced by the pious as a threat to the spiritual goals of the Puritan commonwealth. Despite the diatribes of first and second Great Awakening preachers, economic individualism and materialism continued unabated throughout the seventeenth, eighteenth, and nineteenth centuries. It was the failure of the major voices of the second Great Awakening to resolve the dissonance between religion and world in the economic sphere that gave impetus to the more radical and idiosyncratic attempts by religiously inspired utopianists such as John Humphrey Noyes and the Oneida communists.

The collectivism of the primitive Church provided the model for Noyes's Bible communism. For Noyes, private property was a vestige of an earlier age. The kingdom of heaven on earth would be communist and prosperous. In the age of Christian fulfillment, the sacred and secular realms were merged and the fruits of economic activity would create the heavenly prosperity that was man's destiny. Once the tension between religion and economy was transcended theologically, economic activity became a religious enterprise.

Chapter 3 explores Protestantism's democratic equality of regenerate individuals, and its tension with the political institutions of the day. It also examines the conflict within Protestantism; between its democratic thrust and its rigid social hierarchy and intolerant moral dualism. The primacy of the regeneration of the individual soul and the equality of all before the Mercy Seat were at the core of the second Great Awakening's democratic impulse. But, alongside the democracy of revivalism and revival-inspired Antimasonry stood a religiously conservative wing distrustful of the masses, antagonistic to the economic and political organization of the working class, and opposed to concrete political reforms.

The two conflicts—one between religion and political life, the other within religion—remained unresolved by the second Great Awakening. John Humphrey Noyes realized that the kingdom of heaven on earth would require heavenly political order. The tension between religion and politics was dissolved by his system of "democratic theocracy" instituted at the Oneida Community to unite the universalism of regenerate souls with the aristocracy of spiritual virtuosity and inspiration.

Chapter 4 treats the tension between religion and sex, women, and the family and considers both the religious ambivalence in these areas and the conflict between religion and world. At the core of Protestant prudery is the idea that sexual "excess"—and we shall see the varying definitions of "excess"—led to alienation from religious responsibility, physical drain and deterioration, and neglect of productive social activity. Second Great Awakening preachers incessantly threatened eternal damnation for lustful thoughts and actions, and warned of dire social decay if sexuality was not tightly reined. A considerable body of secular popular literature supported this repressive sexual ideology, but an equally large literature portrayed sex as a satisfying, normal, and healthy activity essential to human well-being.

Protestantism contained its own contradiction over the status of women. Christian misogyny subjugated woman to man as punishment for Eve's temptation of Adam and the subsequent introduction of sin into the world, and provided the ideological legitimation for sexual inequality in the secular sphere. But, by the mid-nineteenth century, the democratic impulse of the second Great Awakening and its benevolent ethos elevated the religious status of women. At revival meetings women prayed and exhorted with men, and seemed more receptive to the emotionalism of the "new measures" and conversion. Women were even more prominent at the smaller prayer meetings and Bible study groups, and in the many missionary, tract, and benevolent societies spawned by the enthusiasms. Championed as representatives of the moral authority of church and home, women were used as foils by revivalists in combat with the religious deterioration and secular corruption they saw accompanying economic growth, industrialism, urbanization, and westward expansion.

While religion expanded women's arena of social action, legal, political, and economic reform lagged far behind. Women's "separate sphere" had crystallized in nineteenth-century popular literature—particularly in the "women's magazines"—and these sexual stereotypes endured. The ideology of demure, submissive, fragile, and emotional femininity was in clear conflict with the practical needs of everyday life. The factory towns, industrializing cities, farms, and frontier demanded and created strong, self-reliant women.

The family itself was also a locus of conflict between religion and world. The industrializing economy and expanding frontier of the nineteenth century weakened the emotional ties and moral authority of the family, and eliminated its role as an economically productive unit. Second Great Awakening preachers demanded the revitalization of the family as a moral force and as the foundation of the commonwealth. Revivalism also divided families. Conversion often split households between the regenerate and unregenerate, or along sectarian lines.

All these tensions remained unresolved by the second Great Awakening, and John Humphrey Noyes grappled with them in his theology and practice of complex marriage. According to Noyes, the new age of Christian fulfillment—in which the kingdom of heaven on earth was a real possibility—required new institutions that corresponded to man's spiritual perfection. Paul's dictum, "in the resurrection they neither marry nor are given in marriage," revealed to Noyes the true familial arrangement: a collective marriage in which each community member was "husband" or "wife" to every other. The moral authority of the family would be extended to the entire community. This collective family would eliminate the selfishness, individualism, and materialism that arose from the conventional family and private property.

Complex marriage included a communism of property and persons. Just as no member could claim monopoly over the use of Oneida Community property, none could claim exclusive right to the love, affection, and sexual favors of any Perfectionist. Rather than alienating the individual from religion and community, sex became a religious sacrament itself, an affirmation of community ideals and solidarity.

Worldly marriage, according to Noyes, was only a small step above slavery. Women were reduced to chattel and were subject to the sexual and childbearing demands of their husbands, no matter how undeserving they might be. Complex marriage would free woman from a life of household drudgery and sexual exploitation. Women and men were equal in religious, intellectual, and social potential and this equality was reflected in the community division of labor and system of status differentiation.

From the seventeenth to the nineteenth century, American intellectual life was dominated by the pulpit. Until the mid-nineteenth century, science served as handmaiden to religion. Science, charged with increasing the understanding of God's creation and his glory, seemed to be consonant with American Protestantism as a whole, save within those sects that rejected all intellectual knowledge. Before science developed an autonomous, professional institutional structure it was dependent upon the religious establishment for its cultural and intellectual legitimacy. Scientists themselves insisted on the harmony between religion and science and censured colleagues whose work challenged Scripture and revelation.

With the growing technical and mathematical sophistication of science in the nineteenth century, it was no longer possible for the layperson and talented amateur to keep up. Their scientific interests were catered to on the less-sophisticated level of lyceums, mechanics' institutes, and popular literature. Scientific organizations and journals began to serve a narrower public, and the social circle of scientists came to include only technically trained professionals. With growing institutional autonomy and the exclusion of amateurs and clergy from the center of scientific activity, science began to generate theories independent of, and often in conflict with, religious justifications.

The thought of John Humphrey Noyes matured in an era when the major scientific and theological voices saw no significant tension between religion and science. In the kingdom of heaven on earth, science was counted on to increase God's glory, to yield generous technical and material improvements for mankind, and to provide the index for man's progressive intellectual improvement and growing spiritual perfection. Community courses and lectures on the physical and natural sciences and mathematics were attended by young and old. Advanced scientific training at Yale or Harvard was available to talented young members of the Oneida Community.

Noyes was convinced that the community's scientific practice would be its crowning religious achievement. The work of Darwin and Galton suggested that the same principles that governed scientific breeding of livestock could be applied to humankind. To this end Noyes introduced "stirpiculture" (from the Latin *stirps*, meaning stem, root, stock, or source), which would reproduce offspring of higher spiritual, intellectual, and physical stature through selective breeding of community members. Science would provide the means to reproduce the community and create the genetic stock for a spiritually perfect humanity.

It seemed that John Humphrey Noyes was rather successful in transcending the tension between religion and world in theology and practice. But it will become apparent that this success was ultimately limited to the theological level. New tensions between religion and economy, democracy, sex, and science arose within Oneida's utopian institution and proved to be the community's undoing.

A prosperous and growing community economy required rational managerial and technical skills that undermined the role of inspiration in business and threatened religious principles. Community business enterprises came to be run by a new generation of youthful managers with a greater appreciation of the "bottom line" than the tenets of Perfectionism.

Noyes's system of "Democratic Theocracy" worked only as long as charisma and religious belief could be counted on to forge consensus. As Noyes aged and his influence waned, the religious indifference and skepticism of Oneida's youth came into the open and undermined community consensus. The delicate balance between democracy and theocracy was upset and "democratic" factions divided the community over loyalty to Noyes, new leadership, and the future of the community.

Because sex was to be a spiritually elevating experience it had to be closely supervised. A system of "ascending fellowship" was instituted to ensure lovemaking spiritually uplifted its partners. Members were encouraged to establish liaisons with their spiritual superiors— i.e., those recognized as more advanced on the path to spiritual perfection—and to make sure their "descending fellowships" did not drain their spiritual "capital." The religious primacy of sex, and community mores and sanctions against sexual selfishness, possessiveness, and exclusive love created a highly regulated community sex life that impeded resolution of sexual competition and jealousy. Ultimately, unresolved sexual discord was sublimated into conflict over the administration and institution of complex marriage.

By sending its brightest young members off to college, the community created two "sciences" at home. Oneida's older generation saw science contributing to God's glory and the understanding of his creations. Lacking technical training, its appreciation of science was limited to the wonders of the physical universe. It accepted the harmony between religion and science. The younger generation of community members was exposed to a different view of science at Yale and Harvard. Mathematics and rigorous scientific reasoning made several key members religious skeptics when belief defied rational proof. The community became divided between those who sought religious salvation and those who pursued scientific rationalism as an independent value.

These internal divisions crippled the community's resistance to external attack and made solutions to internal problems increasingly doubtful. The religious consensus, unity of purpose, and confidence in inspiration that had served so well in the past had crumbled. On January 1, 1881, the Oneida Community divided and reorganized as the Oneida Community, Ltd., a joint-stock company. The boundaries between religion and world had been reestablished and the community's utopian era came to a close.

Part II
Protestantism
and Society
in the United States

2

The Tension
between Religion
and Economy

Max Weber's *The Protestant Ethic and the Spirit of Capitalism* has been a focal point for scholars examining the relationship of Puritanism and capitalist development in colonial America and the young republic, but all have ignored his related essay, "Religious Rejections of the World and Their Directions," which clarifies and qualifies the harmony and conflict between religion and economy elaborated in the more widely cited work.[1] Let us look carefully at how Weber established the tension between religion and economic life in this essay, and how Puritanism fits into the picture. The two central aspects of this relationship that provide religion's social context are the ethic of brotherliness and the rationality of the economic order. Market calculation and the interest struggles of economic actors lie at the heart of Weber's rational economy, and require the evaluation of people, their labor, and products in terms of the most abstract, impersonal common denominator of human life—money.[2] Once the elements of personal social relations are undermined by the cash nexus of rational capitalist economy, the ethic of brotherliness becomes more and more an ethical and practical burden. Only Puritanism and mysticism, which we do not consider in this study, offered the possibility for resolving this tension.

Weber did not see Puritanism as completely consonant with a

worldly economic ethic. First and foremost, the important impulse of Puritanism was religious, but the behavior patterns, the valuative and normative structure, and the annunciation of ascetic Protestantism were conducive to, motivated by, and legitimated through the kind of inner-worldly economic activity that proved important to the accumulation and expansion of capital and the capitalist spirit. The clash of sacred and secular ethics—brotherliness and the demands of a rational economy—gives Puritanism its compromising character. The ethic of "vocation" was critical to Puritanism's compromise because of its rational routinization of all worldly work into serving God's will and as a test of one's state of grace, and because of its renunciation of the universalism of grace. Further, this ethic meant renouncing salvation as a goal attainable by man's efforts. Henceforth salvation could only be interpreted as being arbitrary.

The efficacy of the Puritan "compromise" hinges on its rationalization of economic activity and its unbrotherliness born of the individualized concept of grace. Thus the maturity of capitalism is certainly central in Puritanism's role as "compromiser." The nature of grace and the relationship between human action and salvation can only be derived from and supported by religious sources. The fashion in which Puritanism deals with these religious anxieties—the relation between human action and salvation, and particularly brotherliness and salvation—is also crucial to its efficacy as an agency of compromise. Certainly, in doctrinaire terms, Puritanism provides a possible resolution of the tension between religion and economic life, but Puritanism as a living religion, subject to sacred and secular influence, renders the relationship problematic. Weber did not claim that Puritanism was everywhere successful in overcoming these tensions, only that its promise lay in its theological base. Given the stormy history of Protestantism in America, its wide range of sectarian interpretations and social contexts, one, and certainly Weber, would not anticipate absolute consonance or conflict between capitalism and Puritanism, or unmitigated success or failure in its compromise.

For present purposes, it is necessary to examine the religious and economic context that provided the tension between these two spheres in nineteenth-century America, a tension that surfaced early despite, if not due to, Puritanism's worldly ethic of vocation.

The Contradictions of Puritan Colonial Life:
The Jeremiad, "Vocation," and Economic Activity

Perry Miller detects an emerging uneasiness and rising anxiety in a
sermon of Richard Mather, the principal architect of the Cambridge
Reform by which in 1648 orthodox New England published its distinctive constitution of church governance. On April 10, 1657,
Mather exhorted his congregation and New England to hold fast to
the Westminster Confession and stand by the ecclesiastical polity in
his moving "A Farewell-Exhortation to the Church and People of
Dorchester in New England." Behind his admonition lurks a specter
that suggests mounting Puritan anxiety about the future:

It is true the conditions of many amongst you . . . is such as necessarily puts
you to have much employment about the things of this life, and to labor with
care and paines taking in the works of husbandry and other worldly business
for the maintenance of your selves & your families, the Lord having laid this
burden on man . . . & experience shews that it is an easy thing in the middest
of worldly business to lose the life and Power of Religion, that nothing there
should be left but only the external form, as it were the carcass or shell,
worldliness having eaten out the kernell, and having consumed the very soul
and life of godliness.[3]

The physical struggle and the economic demands of the New
World deflected the spirit, and the temptations of economic growth
and prosperity would certainly test the resolve of the Puritan soul.
New England provided the opportunity for a fresh start toward
Christian community, but it was not a "new" world in any religious
sense of the world: it was the same "old" world of sin and struggle
that required constant vigilance.

These worldly anxieties over God-ordained work in the world and
the temptations of affluence forged the first native literary genre: the
clerical jeremiad. A subtle yet eloquent sermon exploring sin and
regeneration, the jeremiad became the centerpiece during colonial
periods of collective trial, humiliation, and deliverance. These rituals
of confession told a story of a society founded by men dedicated to
sacred, eternal principles slowly undermined by involvement with
the mundane affairs of the world. "They constitute a chapter in the
emergence of the capitalist mentality, showing how intelligence
copes with—or more cogently, how it fails to cope with—a change it
simultaneously desires and abhors."[4]

While venting the frustrations of virtuous intent, jeremiads created a ritual form that crystallized the conflicts between religion and

economic life and strung the ethical tightrope on which the righteous
Puritan had to walk. Jeremiads offered no real solutions; they only
inaugurated periodic collective expressions of guilt and ritualized
redemptive activity. The jeremiad and humiliation were only a temporary salve that never attempted to confront and resolve the contradictions of Puritan life. They only raised them to the level of collective awareness.

Although the ethic of the vocation and predestination had a strong
individualizing force on the early American Puritan psyche, the concept of the calling also included strong communal elements. Protestant divines such as William Perkins and John Cotton tempered individualism with exhortations to serve the public weal. The purpose of
civil as well as religious life was to serve faith and God. For Perkins, a
Cambridge theologian, the individual pursuit of one's calling was insufficient ground for worldly activity directed toward the glory of
God. The calling could be meaningful only within a collective Christian context. This involved the joining of vocations, obediently and
faithfully, to serve God's glory.[5] The communal ethos of the calling
fostered a clearly defined hierarchical conception of social structure
in which each family had a specified position. But the economic
success that followed diligent work in one's vocation, once it spread
beyond those of inherited wealth and status, threatened the God-
ordained social categories and structure of the Puritan community.
Social mobility did more than just test the state of one's grace, it
could also signify the defiance of a God-ordained calling. The unprecedented growth and scale of New England economic activity
that began in the mid-seventeenth century, and the increased need to
evaluate situations in terms of economic criteria, severely threatened
the social and communal aspects of the Protestant ethic of vocation.
As New England merchants prospered, orthodox clergy feared de-
clension. Sermons began to plead for "unity" and "order" in the face
of changing conditions and a social structure in flux. Economic mobility was jarring the staid social structure that had its ideological
roots in Puritan orthodoxy. Downward mobility was as problematic
as success, particularly when hardworking farmers, who appeared to
all as virtuous and upright, declined under the economic thumb of
merchants, bankers, and shippers.

The calling of commerce left little leisure for meditation on the
close distinction between works as a condition of the Covenant of
Grace and works in the Arminian heresy.[6] By 1730, the religious

principles underpinning work were fading, and work itself became perceived as an ethical matter.

Along with creeping materialism and the internal contradictions of Puritanism, seventeenth-century New England began to experience a growing secularization of polity and of social and economic issues. As the secular state became central, New England did not abandon Protestantism as the ethical and moral template for polity, but Christian liberties, prescriptions, and proscriptions came to be guaranteed by civil law rather than authoritarian religious fiat.

Clerical denunciations of the excesses of wealth and commerce did little to endear the ministry to the rising merchant class that was to supplant it in the political arena. The first Great Awakening also stirred up antiministerial sentiment and devalued the orthodox ministry's institutional and charismatic authority.

The Puritan Commonwealth vs. Secular Economic Individualism

The cultural landscape of New England had become severely fragmented. Puritanism itself had become a spiritual centrifuge, the disparate elements separating into sectarianism, and mutual accusations of apostasy and heresy keeping them apart. As early as 1650 Congregationalism, Presbyterianism, Anabaptism, and Arminianism were split on fundamental religious questions such as free will, the calling, predestination, preparation for salvation, infant baptism, and the Half-Way Covenant.[7] The Protestant ethic urged all to work hard and to accomplish in the world. "The only way of living acceptably to God was not to surpass worldly morality in monastic asceticism, but solely through the fulfillment of the obligations imposed on the individual by his position in the world. That was his calling."[8] But the social obligation of the Puritan ethic—the joining of callings in communal effort demanded by Puritan divines—was collapsing under the weight of the individualizing elements of inner-worldly asceticism. The first Great Awakening (c. 1720–1760) was, in several respects, an attempt to resuscitate a Puritan communalism choked by economic individualism; it called for a return to an earlier age of Puritan determinacy, which never existed, but was still the heart of the American promise. The details of the first Great Awakening are of no immediate concern to us here and have been recounted by many.[9] What is important are the main targets of the revivalist attack—the calling and economic activity.

Alongside the internal anomaly of the calling, other secular forces were at work deteriorating the communal aspects of Puritanism, hastening the decline of spiritual values, and accelerating economic individualism. Settlement, expansion, and economic opportunity were wooing the New England colonist away from the ideal of the Puritan commonwealth and toward the economic individualism and self-aggrandizement of nascent American capitalism.

Land business, perhaps more than any other colonial economic activity, involved all walks of life in the private pursuit of gain and the violation of the Puritan commonwealth. Early expansion of New England settlements generally corresponded to the growing needs of a local agricultural and artisan population. It was natural that rank and status, the main props of the social order according to Scripture and English custom, were respected. Sufficient land would have to be apportioned to allow the gentleman, yeoman, artisan, or laborer to maintain his proper station. By the early eighteenth century, the auctioneer's gavel replaced rank and settlement requisites, and anticipated revenues for provincial and personal coffers undermined the old religious and social ends. Not only were whole towns in western New England bought by absentee Boston, Salem, and Connecticut Valley merchants and financiers; ordinary farmers enthusiastically speculated on acreage that they and their families could not possibly work.

Evangelical preachers lost confidence in the ability of the calling to integrate secular and religious life and they confronted those who abandoned the spiritual and communal aspects of the calling in favor of its mundane economic ethic. The wealth of economic opportunity and the expansion of the sphere of social activity that required decision making based solely on rational, calculable, material considerations warned Great Awakening preachers of a snowballing secularism. Their attack on the spiritual and social abuses of the secularized calling encompassed nearly all economic activity. Temptation, covetousness, and pride were as much a part of economy as were trade, commerce, and profit. Once the calling's capacity for the integration of social and spiritual life was subverted in the marketplace the evangelical clergy lashed out at selfishness and greed as the greatest sins of the age.

Theologically, the first Great Awakening appealed to an already eclipsed idealized tradition. Lacking the primary spiritual commitment to the Puritan "tradition," and resurrected in a radically different economic context than its original one, it could only draw forth a utopian "traditionalism" as a device for exhortation and psychological flagellation. Although the "new measures" of revivalism brought significant changes to American religious life, they did not succeed in stemming the tide of economic individualism. Revivalism's lasting result ran counter to its avowed aims. Rather than uniting America under the umbrella of Puritan consensus, it furthered the fragmentation of the social order by aggravating sectarian differences and pitting adherents of the new against adherents of the old.

The North's Industrial Explosion, 1790–1860

Economic individualism continued unabated during and after the Great Awakening. By 1730 colonial settlement had hardly advanced 100 miles inland. Between 1730 and 1890, the frontier advanced by tremendous leaps. The apparent limitlessness of North American agricultural resources and the colonial disregard for conservation engendered a "wagon-wheel" mentality among many settlers. The promise of greener pastures to replace stubborn or exhausted soil enticed many to pull up stakes several times within a generation for the trek westward.

According to Robert E. Brown,[10] there was little significant modernization of economic life in the eighteenth century. In general, technology and farm productivity stood still. The standardization of parts and mass production of firearms certainly foretold the coming of an industrial age, but this was not the work of New England merchants seeking new outlets for and sources of capital. Inventors such as Eli Whitney, Simeon North, and others, embodying yet transcending the "jack-of-all-trades" tradition of early American craftsmanship, were responsible for these technological advances. In the South, increased plantation production was a result of greater acreage tilled for tobacco and the adjustment of both labor and land to plantation culture. In the North there emerged stable aristocratic elites dedicated to maintaining a particular gentlemanly life-style traditional of the English domain. In Pennsylvania, wealthy merchants and large landowners of the eastern counties dominated provincial economic and political life. Along the fertile Hudson Valley, large land grants begat a feudal squirearchy that, allied with wealthy merchants and New York City real-estate speculators, controlled New York's political and economic life. The economic interests of New England were no different as they sought to get in on the ground floor of an aristocratic tradition. If the upper class lacked a native cultural and social style, the growth of the imperial establishment between 1690 and 1760 offered first-hand examples of the perquisites and privileges that came with powerful establishment modeled after the ancient regime.

Between 1790 and 1860 "the East was discovering its Utopia in an industrial capitalist order."[11] For the United States as a whole, the factory had virtually replaced household manufacturing by 1860. Some vestiges of household production remained in the 1830s but home industry had already been rendered insignificant by the factory system. In New England, the Middle States, Maryland, and the Northwest territories, the household system had been discontinued by 1860.[12] Scientific and technological development accelerated in this period; westward expansion yielded the natural resources necessary for sustained industrial growth; peace with England and in Europe revived immigration; and turnpikes, toll roads, canals, and other internal improvements built by immigrants permitted the expansion and integration of local markets into a national economy.

The eighteenth century did bring about a significant change in the fashion in which business was done. In the seventeenth century, the volume of trade was relatively small and personal relationships were predominant. Brothers, sons, and in-laws acted as colonial agents for European relatives. Credit was equally personal, generally extended from one community member to another rather than through institutions. Buyers, to ensure supply, often extended credit to producers. By the middle of the eighteenth century, New England trade with the Caribbean was so well standardized that merchants need not fret over their cargo. Administration and management became more important. One had to retain reliable and, above all, capable men, managers who were to increasing degree bound only by mutual material interest.[13]

The revolution of the nineteenth century was also a social one, but the economic tasks at hand overshadowed concern for the social and cultural disjunctions and distortions brought about by the factory system. It was an order whose preeminent value was economic progress. The same institutional structure that had watched the play of economic forces in the preindustrial eighteenth century remained in the laissez-faire balcony for the next act. The factory worker, freed from the traditionalism of farm and family production, was bound anew in the time and work discipline of the shop.[14]

When the government involved itself in the economy, it did so in a fashion that, for the most part, created an environment favorable to industrialization. The tariff was so important to the nascent industrial classes that, as Joseph Dorfman has found, the laboring class could be held "hostage" over it:

> The iron-masters, Peter Cooper and his son-in-law, Abram S. Hewitt, declared in the columns of the *New York Journal of Commerce* that, if the iron industry is to compete successfully against British labor, either wages must be reduced to the British level of mere subsistence or a suitable tariff must be provided. If wages are reduced then the iron-workers' children must be imprisoned in a cotton factory as soon as they can walk and become almost as soul-less as the machinery they guide.[15]

By the 1830s, legislatures enacted statutes making incorporation readily available on a small or large scale. Banking and finance followed westward expansion and paralleled economic growth. Boston, Philadelphia, and especially New York grew in financial and commercial stature, becoming the nerve centers of American domestic and international economy. Government carefully fostered economic growth by permitting easy incorporation and expansion of banking—in contrast to earlier state charters and monopolies—and it provided little regulatory control.

Although there has been a significant labor literature in the United States from the 1820s and the attempt at organizing factory labor began in the earliest New England textile mills, the first significant factory legislation was not introduced until 1848 when Pennsylvania passed a ten-hour work-day law applying primarily to children. Similar proposals in Massachusetts were opposed by manufacturers and were killed in legislative committee.[16]

With industrialization came urbanization. As the population of the United States increased from 3.9 million in 1790 to 31.5 million in 1860, the number of urban places increased from 24 to 392, and the urban population rose from 202,000 to 6.2 million.[17] With large concentrations of population came a host of urban problems that America previously had not had to confront.

With the economic developments of the eighteenth and nineteenth centuries began the decline of local economies and markets, the depersonalization of commercial and credit transactions and the rise of institutional credit, the decline of the family and household as a significant productive entity, and the transition to factory labor. The factory transformed the social character of labor by chaining productive activity to the rhythms of clock and machine rather than by valuing craftsmanship and tradition. Economic values became the preeminent motivating force.

Lest one get the idea that 1790 to 1860 was a period of constant economic expansion and prosperity, we must note that the economy stumbled several times. The embargo of 1807 led to the collapse of domestic prices and widespread unemployment. The severity of the economic dislocation was finally alleviated by the Non-Intercourse Act of 1809 which reopened trade with all except Britain and France. The Panic of 1837 burst the bubble of speculative fever that swept the American economy. Jackson's Specie Circular of 1836 demanded payment in specie rather than in paper money for public lands—of which 20 million acres had been sold that year. Inflated paper pyramids previously supported by the dubious credit of speculators and wildcat banks collapsed. This crisis wrought the collapse of the canal-building craze, and at least 33,000 commercial and industrial failures involving losses of $440 million.[18]

Juggling the Christian Calling and Laissez-Faire Political Economy

The clergy and religious minded of the early nineteenth century were not blind to the excesses, cruelties, and immoralities of industrial capitalism but, for the most part, the clerical political economy that developed between 1830 and 1850 reinforced private property, laissez-faire, antiunionism, and the instruments of capitalist industrial society with the immutable laws of God and his inviolate will.

Although Adam Smith is well remembered for placing ministers among the ranks of unproductive labor, his other ideas were adopted by clerical political economists such as Rev. John McVickar (*Outlines of Political Economy*, 1825). The root of evil in manufacturing, thought McVickar, was the neglect of the education of the youth of the working force. Where parental affection was insufficient, the power of law should be brought to bear, regulating the age and working hours of children and making provisions for sufficient education. Benevolent as it appears, the fundamental thrust of clerical political economy appears in McVickar's thoughts on the poor laws. McVickar, with other Malthusians, found poverty to be a reflection of the moral qualities of the individual rather than a product of an economic system. The true causes of poverty were ignorance and vice. Any relief that provided physical sustenance alone further ruined the moral character of the poor. The best poor laws would provide for education, well-regulated penitentiaries, and restraints on intemperance.[19]

Francis Wayland—minister, university president, lecturer on political economy, and author of popular textbooks on the subject—was considered by many to be the "Ricardo of the Evangelists" for his melding of laissez-faire political economy with the stewardship of wealth. Wealth and property, in Wayland's mind, were gifts from God and people can do what they please with them. But humans are accountable to God, and prosperity is bestowed by him as a means to happiness that is to be bestowed on others, not retained for personal gratification.

Wayland tried to juggle the moral laws of the Christian calling and the economic laws of the British classical political economists, but his notion of stewardship and the divine source of economic laws did little more than provide a religious legitimation of economic individualism, laissez-faire, and the single-minded pursuit of wealth.[20] The "hidden hand" of the market was none other than God's. Poverty and the wretchedness born of the factory system were not abominations in God's eyes but elements in his economic system. Like McVickar, Wayland saw poverty and the suffering of labor as the result of personal moral failures rather than economic vices, with a justifiable place in God's scheme. The divine plan demanded the division of property and wealth rather than economic equality and communal ownership. The government has no right to levy protective tariffs, alter the value of specie, or "oppress" the banks. Charity should only be extended to the afflicted. Other clerical economists and revivalists denounced trade unions and strikes, which artificially raised wages and crippled capitalists who provided work. They imagined them as led by foreigners and atheists, and believed that unions tended toward secrecy and class antagonism and invaded the rights of employers, farmers, and nonunion workmen.[21]

The Puritan covenant had been transformed into an economic system through which God's will would be done. Just as the Puritans of the seventeenth century could only blame themselves for their misfortune, the indigent and the working poor were held responsible for their own fate, and the industrial class was exonerated. In general, the early critics of industrialism viewed poverty in moral terms. There would always be poor; one's Christian duty lay in morally elevating them. Only the most radical—Francis Wright, Robert Dale Owens, Albert Brisbane, the German communists, and English Chartists in America—questioned the fundamental institutions of

capitalism, private property, and labor as a commodity. Socialism
and "Owenism" were generally condemned as attempts to sustain
atheism and their exponents denounced them as alien and infidel.

The Second Great Awakening and the
Contradiction of "Christian" Capitalism

Charles C. Cole, Jr., found the evangelists of the second Great Awakening (1820–1860) divided by contrary sets of religious ideas.[22]
They saw a need for a conscious effort to subordinate things of the
world to the things of the spirit and to restore religious affairs to a
position above that of mundane economic matters, but they also
gave evidence of a strong impulse toward the protection of property,
the defense of capitalism, and the appeasement of the monied classes
that could support their many benevolent evangelical enterprises.
This dichotomy was, at various times, expressed by the same
individual.

The major religious leaders offered little more than "moral support" for the downtrodden. The blows of poverty and the hardness
of heart of early American capitalism were countered with religious
compassion and a critique of the morality of the poor. This combination of religiously inspired commiseration and laissez-faire political
economy that blamed the victims and rejected interfering with "natural" or "eternal" economic laws and institutions was the fundamental contradiction of "Christian" capitalism.

Evangelical leaders spoke out often on economic matters. Charles
Grandison Finney, Lyman Beecher, Horace Bushnell, Francis Wayland, and Albert Barnes all advocated the subordination of money-
making to the seeking of salvation. Barnes represented the feelings of
the revivalist ministry in declaring:

The love of gain . . . is still our besetting sin. This passion goads our country-
men, and they forget all other things. . . . They go for gold, and they wander
over the prairie, they fell the forest, they ascend the stream in search of it, and
they trample down the law of the Sabbath, and soon, too, forget the laws of
honesty and fairdealing, in the insatiable love of gain.[23]

Finney brought the world to task because its business was governed by the maxim of "supreme and unmixed selfishness." The everyday commercial practices of business as usual were inconsistent
with God's commands. "Looking out for number one" was selfish,
greedy, prideful, and ungodly. Despite the radical religious rhetoric,

Finney, like Lyman Beecher and Horace Bushnell, was an economic conservative. All these men assumed that economic laws were just as rigid as God's laws and tampering with them was just as improper.

For many of the revivalists there was nothing inherently sinful or immoral about economic activity in the new industrial age. Reform of the capitalist system was not in order; conversion of the capitalist was the key. While the northern evangelists had their greatest success with the rural laboring and agricultural classes, they also enthusiastically pursued the conversion of the monied class. Even before Finney's first revival success in an urban area (Rochester, New York, 1830), he looked forward to bringing his brand of religion to the upper class of New York City, Boston, and Philadelphia. In New York, with the aid of the Tappan family, Finney carried philanthropy to a new height. Converted capitalists were needed to finance revivals and the many tract and missionary societies spawned by the enthusiasms. The more volatile causes of abolition and antislavery also sought philanthropic support and received significant electoral support in northern areas singed by the fires of revivalism.[24]

The northern evangelists had further reason to welcome industrialization. They were quick to recognize the potential of the factory system as a source of converts, providing an organized setting for revivals. In isolated incidents, revivalists literally invaded factories and shut them down for revival meetings. Factory owners often invited revivalists to their shops; their preaching within the factory walls helped bolster the capitalist system.

By and large, the evangelists offered moral support for the social and economic improvement of the downtrodden. When it came to substantive measures such as poor relief, factory legislation, or the eight- or ten-hour day, they balked and resorted to clerical laissez-faire. Only the most radical ministers such as William Ellery Channing and Orestes A. Brownson, and the utopian communalists John Humphrey Noyes, William Keil (founder of the Aurora and Bethel communities), the Shakers, the German and Swedish "primitive" Christian sects, and Swedenborgianism raised Christian alternatives to capitalist industrialism.

Although the evangelists of the second Great Awakening offered little more than conversion for the amelioration of the sins of capitalist economy, the communal collective experience of the protracted revival meeting, evening prayer meetings, and the intense emotional sermon and methods of revivalists offered a communal balm to the atomizing consequences of industrialization and westward expansion. Revivalism offered universal conversion. The "spirit" could dwell and swell in the heart that had been opened and had sincerely renounced sin and damnation. Temporary as the immediate results often were—communities sometimes asked revivalists to return when enthusiasm waned after the first revival—they were attempts at creating communities of the converted in opposition to the fragmentation of a society of sinners.

The revivalists of the second Great Awakening confronted the same problems left by the failure of the first Great Awakening. The Puritan "community of saints" could not be revived by the first Great Awakening but conversion became the focus of religious life. Emotional intensity, a perceived cleansing of spirit, and the apparent communal embrace of religion offered a measure of surety that the predeterminism of Puritanism denied.

The ascension of economic over spiritual values continued after the first and second Great Awakenings, and their leaders faced the paradox of simultaneously despising, embracing, and using wealth. The immensity of the task of saving souls required enormous financial support which meant preachers had to court the monied class and take care not to bite the hand that fed them.

The conflict between religion and economy merged over the issues of individualism and community. The contradiction between capitalism and the Christian spirit remained unresolved by the major religious thrust of the second Great Awakening. The mainstream of revival religion straddled these issues, providing radical rhetoric, yet legitimating the capitalist system. Their economic ideology was one of contradictions. It was a "Christian" capitalism, benevolent yet laissez-faire, seeking communal affirmation while sanctifying private property and the pursuit of wealth. The combination of radical religious doctrine and conservative political economy sought to eliminate the conflict between Christianity and capitalism but left that tension intact. Revivalism did succeed in forging a historic alliance between fundamentalist religion and economic conservatism that is significant to this day. A far more adventurous attempt to resolve the tension between religion and world was made by John Humphrey Noyes.

The Economic Ideology of John Humphrey Noyes

We have already noted that the religious leap into utopia requires the unification of religion and world. In the northeastern United States during the nineteenth century, this meant (1) resolving the internal contradictions of the "vocation"; (2) reversing the ascension of economic and material concerns over spiritual values and resolving the competition between religion and economy for the attention, time, and energy of the individual; and (3) resolving the tension between the economic individualism of laissez-faire capitalism and the religious ethos of brotherliness, universal love, and Christian community.

John Humphrey Noyes believed that heretofore unprecedented economic prosperity would accompany the spiritual elevation promised in the kingdom of heaven on earth. Including economic salvation and communal luxury dissolved the internal contradictions of the Protestant ethic of vocation. Hard, disciplined, rationally calculated, worldly work would develop the Christian character and build a heavenly economy, liberating humanity from material want. Rather than threatening religion, economic progress became a religious mission. Spiritual progress was to be the tree that bore the fruit of economic prosperity.

Mere economic reform and religious revivalism were insufficient for the cultivation of Noyes's religious orchard—a new stock was required. The discovery that humanity lived in the age of Christian consumption gave the spiritually advanced the freedom to abandon the institutional structures and social conventions appropriate to an earlier religious era. To this end Noyes and the Oneida Community introduced "Bible communism." Striking at what he thought to be the heart of economic individualism and the obsessive attachment to private property and wealth, Noyes abolished conventional marriage and familial arrangements and created complex marriage. By breaking the boundaries of exclusive love and instituting a communal marriage and family, Noyes was convinced he could level the obstacles that prevented unselfish love of God, universal love of man, and a Christian economic order based on the communism of Paul and the primitive Church.

Once humanity's spiritual nature was further developed and the communal basis of economy and family established, true brotherliness and collective ownership of property and management of production would eliminate the inequities and cruelties of American industrialism. Religion and world had been merged in an ascetic ethic in which religious values generate the promised prosperity of the kingdom of heaven on earth.

3
Religion and
Democracy

Max Weber saw the brotherly ethic of universalistic salvation religions in acute tension with the political orders of the world.[1] The more rational the political order becomes, the greater the tension that develops from the demands of brotherliness. The bureaucratic state apparatus discharges justice according to rational rules without regard to person, hence without hate or love. The state's absolute end is to safeguard or change the external distribution of power, a goal that must seem meaningless to any universalist religion of salvation. As the state claims a monopoly of the legitimate use of violence, the success and threat of force ultimately depend upon power relationships, not on an ethical notion of "right."

Aside from this inherent tension, politics may come into direct competition with religious ethics. The threat of violence in itself is capable of producing a strong fellowship opposed to the religious community. In the face of such a threat the brotherliness of a group bound in war must appear devalued in a brotherly religion. As the threat of violence and war solves the problem of the meaning of death, it must appear to a religious ethic of brotherliness as a glorification of fratricide. The heroic ethos of death in war is a direct competition with charisma and the direct experience of communion with God.

Once again Weber finds in this tension a special kind of a resolution in Puritanism and mysticism. The Puritan resolution is a result of a positive ascetic ideology. The fixed and revealed commandments of God are to be imposed upon the world by the ways of the world. The mystical attitude is radically antipolitical and can best be expressed by the doctrine "resist no evil" and, then, "turn the other cheek." All other solutions are full of compromises and presuppositions that appear as dishonest or unacceptable to the ethic of brotherliness. The ascetic and mystic position may also take on a revolutionary aspect. Such a stance arises when the asceticist is capable of opposing an absolute "divine" law to the wicked orders of the world, and when the mystic is led to the conclusion that the laws and political order of the world do not apply to people who are assured in their obsession with God. Both of these resolutions were utilized by the Oneida Community.

American Protestantism and Democracy: The Convergence of Ideals

American democracy is connected to two different but related themes: a realistic conception and a romantic ideal. Realistic democracy regularly included caucuses, log-rolling, individual struggle for office, and regional sparring for political and economic advantage. This conception was personified by Martin Van Buren, the chief architect of the Democratic party that elected Jackson president. Romantic democracy was a notion including a "cluster of ideas and ideals that, taken together, make up a national faith which, although unrecognized as such, had the power of a state religion." The central ideas were derived for the most part from classical Greece, taking new shape and configuration in America.[2]

Fundamental to the American conception of democratic faith are three doctrines, the first being the idea that beneath society—its culture and institutions—there exists a law that men did not make. For the individual this meant the principles on which to found a worthy life, and for society it meant a prescription for an order within which individuals may grow in understanding and virtue. This notion of a "fundamental law" as it existed in nineteenth-century America had two different origins and emphases: the idea of natural law, derived from Plato and developed further by Enlightenment philosophers; and the belief in moral law, from Moses through the Judeo-Christian tradition. Natural law comprised an urge toward justice as a principle rather than a code. Justice in society is the counterpart of order in nature. From nature itself, through natural law, comes the strain toward justice that, when made the guide of life, becomes the health of the soul. The Judeo-Christian tradition reflects the other principle of abstract justice: the moral is the will of God. Justice Joseph Story, in his *Commentaries on the Constitution of the United States* (1873), melded the two, expressing a basic doctrine of a natural law that was acceptable to both those guided by reason and those who found their direction in Scripture: "The rights of conscience, are, indeed, beyond the just reach of human power. They are given by God and cannot be encroached upon by human authority without criminal disobedience of the precepts of natural as well as revealed religion."[3]

The second doctrine crucial to the American conception of democratic faith focused on the free and responsible individual. Men of the nineteenth century thought of society as an aggregate of discrete individuals who were the ultimate governors of the nation.

And finally, the notion of the mission of America was critical. Liberty had been established by deity in an empty western continent so that, freed from European traditions, it might flourish and become an inspiration to the rest of the world.[4]

America was hardly a place where one could sit and wait for the fulfillment of such a promise. The uncompromising Calvinist conception of the world was well adapted to the struggle of the pioneers against the wilderness. The hard conditions of life required continuous labor, and the system of John Calvin came close to sanctifying work, hard constructive work, and the reinvestment of its rewards. Once the tension of the frontier struggle relaxed a bit and life became easier, Americans began to chafe at the harsh ethos of Calvinism.

The central appeal of evangelism during the first Great Awakening lay in the individual's winning freedom from bondage. Before conversion, people were held by the shackles of sin that would only be broken when they knelt before the Mercy Seat. There was a distinct shift in emphasis from Calvin's preoccupation with a monarch-god, to evangelical emphasis on Jesus, the divine man. The central theme of the teachings of Jonathan Edwards and his votaries was "liberty [went] to the man from whose limbs the fetters of sin have fallen." Once again, one theme of the romantic conception of democratic faith was the doctrine of the free individual and the progress of man from necessary external restraint by man-made laws toward individual liberty founded on self-control. As Gabriel notes, "so great is the similarity that the doctrine of liberty seems but a secular version of its counterpart in evangelical Protestantism."[5]

Thus far we have only found parallels and consonance between democratic ideals and Protestantism in America. Although a causal nexus between the Protestant worldview and American democracy cannot be entertained, we may still observe a strong democratic thrust in Protestant theology.

American Protestantism and Democracy: Antinomianism, Revivalism, and the Free Individual

Within Puritanism we find contrasting support for and opposition to democratic principles. On the one hand, Puritanism posited the equality of all people before God. Certainly only the elect few would be elevated, but those saints were to be found among all classes. The deepest bond between Puritanism and democracy was the common respect both held for the individual, regardless of his or her place in the social, political, ecclesiastical, or economic order. On the other hand, Puritanism provided a political antithesis to the democratic ethos. Its emphasis on the sovereignty of God, its disposition toward a divinely sanctioned theocratic state, and the sanctification of a favored few were supportive of an aristocratic, hierarchical social structure. Its intolerance and insistence on harmony and consensus in both political and religious matters left an indelible mark on the Massachusetts town meeting. Here, consensus was expected ethically and empirically. Not only was dissension immoral in religious terms, it was also illegitimate and a threat to political community.[6]

To further understand this dialectic of democracy and religion it is useful to keep in mind the broad trend of religious organization and activity since the Reformation: the transformation of the spiritual and ideological apprehension of the Protestant faith from sacerdotal to evangelical. Sacrament, formal theology, centralized organization, and a hierarchy of clergy imposed from above have declined through a process of institutional adaptation to new worldly exigencies and as lay influence has burgeoned. Conversion and justification through profession of faith, morals, and ethics have grown along with the congregational and presbyterian mode of organization. This was not an introduction of new elements, but rather a subtle change of emphasis. Evangelicism was a minority voice that had become dominant by 1850.[7]

The decline of the official clergy and the rise of the laity meant more than democratization of American Protestantism's institutional structure; it also raised significant questions of religious belief. We cannot be content with elaborating Puritanism's "ideal" aspects. For our purposes we must delve into the substance of the debates within Puritanism, chiefly the conflict over "preparation" and antinomianism. We find these issues in the theological triangle of Thomas Hooker, John Cotton, and Anne Hutchinson. Their division prefigures some of the fundamental issues that culminated in the first Great Awakening and the work of Jonathan Edwards.[8]

In the early decades of the seventeenth century, Thomas Hooker and his disciples became involved in an elaborate study of what they considered to be the "preparatory" steps to conversion. Hooker posited chronological phases of conversion, establishing the "order" of God's proceedings. In the probationary period, God first removes the resistance of the soul by an irresistible operation. The soul then becomes a passive power, disposed to spiritual work. The propensity for spiritual good works in "preparation" for salvation comes not from within us, but not without our participation. The "prepared" person was not merely a conduit of God's spiritual work, he or she was the vital nexus between spirit and action.

Most New England leaders followed Hooker despite attacks from England contending that "preparation" depreciated grace, because it could be done by the unregenerate. John Cotton, "dean" of the sacred college by virtue of his position as "teacher" of the First Church in Boston, stood as a notable exception to those supporting Hooker. The activist implications of "preparation" did not sit well with his Calvinist inclinations. The span between nature and grace, insisted Cotton, was unbridgeable: man was passive in his regeneration. What Hooker saw as "preparation," Cotton saw as consequential to salvation. Anne Hutchinson concluded that Cotton alone was teaching the true covenant of grace and she split New England society by accusing all others of preaching a covenant of works. That works have nothing to do with justification, that they offer no "evidence" of salvation, that man can only wait on Christ, and that a true saint might continually live in sin, were at the center of her thought. What finally destroyed her was her conviction that saints could, and did, receive direct revelation from the Holy Ghost.

Hutchinson was sentenced to banishment by the General Court of Massachusetts in November 1637. Throughout the continuing debate and proceedings, she clung to a pillar of establishment, claiming she was merely supporting Cotton's doctrine—he would have to be dealt with too. Cotton finally bowed to the pressure of the "preparation" majority, which restored the appearance of orthodox consensus, and Hutchinson's case was lost. Because Hutchinson was defeated and Cotton ceded, the New England mind became irrevocably committed to the idea of "preparation" and the place of works in salvation. Although the book on Hutchinson was closed and Cotton in the future offered only occasional token resistance, the same issue resurfaced in a slightly altered form in the debate between Arminianism and Calvinism's greatest defender, Jonathan Edwards.

Arminianism, with its doctrine of freedom of the will, seeped into American religious life by way of the Anglican clergy and European rationalism. Its doctrine of individual responsibility meshed well with the New England experience. Townspeople could clearly see and feel the neighborly aid, friendliness, and good will of their fellow settlers and began to seriously doubt the Calvinist insistence on human depravity. Arminianism offered an attractive alternative. The elect were not prechosen; a righteous life and good works would lead to salvation. Striking at predestination, Arminianism further undercut the already enervated orthodox Calvinism. The first Protestant reformers asserted the right to individual interpretation of Scripture; the Arminians gave the individual complete responsibility for his or her salvation.

The anti-Calvinist elements of Arminianism and antinomianism were critical to their strong democratic impulse. Antinomian rejection of the Calvinist commitment to human depravity provided the foundation for the idea of spiritual and political perfectability; it meshed well with the secular philosophy of progress and resonated with American democracy's utopian promise to save the world from autocratic oppression. Furthermore, the doctrine of freedom of will harmonized with the democratic ideal of the free individual. We will see the democratic thrust of antinomianism reappear later in the "new measures" of the second Great Awakening.

For the defenders of Calvinism the whole metaphysical structure of the old order depended on facing Arminianism. Jonathan Edwards took as his task the destruction of the "Arminian heresy," attacking its theological, philosophical, and logical structures. Holding fast to the doctrine of human depravity and predetermined election by the sovereign will of God, Edwards harkened back to an already dated religious absolutism and was out of step with secular changes in New England life. The measure of political freedom, the economic success and material comfort gained by the colonists, the townspeople's visible mutual support, and middle-class experience and expectations all clashed with "fire and brimstone" sermons that preached man's inner darkness and his hellish fate. The belief in the social and spiritual progress of man seemed to calm the fears of middle-class "sinners in the hands of an angry God."

The sermons of Jonathan Edwards occasionally referred to the status distinctions, privileges, and different pursuits within community life, but Edwards submerged these differences in the universal gift of conversion through which all the regenerate will be embraced by Christ. Those remaining in the "natural" state—the unregenerate —will suffer the eternal torment of hell. The leveling of humanity was reserved for the afterlife. All worldly distinctions of wealth, status, and works would be overturned by conversion.[9]

By coming to the defense of Calvinism, Edwards delivered it a lethal blow. Unchangeable human depravity and the explicit horrors of hell would no longer be broadly entertained in New England, and his revolutionary insistence on conversion as the sole ground of admission to communion finished the old theocratic system that had debated the Half-Way Covenant for a century. Conversion held promise, though it came not as a consequence of a person's works but as God's gift. Edwards failed to revive Calvinism, but the passion and zeal of his sermons and the centrality of conversion influenced many other preachers, and his support for the Great Awakening furthered the cause of revivalism.[10]

The conversion experience and the religious feelings that arose out of it wrested religion from the clergy, congregation, and ritual, and substituted an intense personal relationship with God: neither the blessing of intermediaries nor church membership was needed. All the saved could do was open their hearts and await God's gift. The religious fervor of the camp meeting and conversion spread throughout the colonies and restored waning church membership. Filling the churches, however, did not restore Puritanism's clerical hierarchy. Ministers thereafter served at the pleasure of the congregation rather than of the synod, and the laity would take greater control of local religious life.

The fundamental legacy of the first Great Awakening for later waves of religious enthusiasm was its substitution of conversion for Puritan predestination as the alpha and omega of religious life, and the survival of the doctrine of freedom of the will. The second Great Awakening further dismantled Calvinist predestination. The central thrust became the role of man and the means he, or God, might use in the regeneration of the soul. Once again the question of the freedom of will took center stage.

The Wesleyan Methodists accepted freedom of the will far earlier than other denominations, and New England went through tortuous struggles over it. If conversion is possible by an act of will, given God's grace, then all things are possible. Not only can the individual spirit be renovated, society at large can be regenerated by the power of human will in harmony with God's will. Charles Grandison Finney took the question of free will one step further, abandoning that part of the Westminister Confession that pertained to passive regeneration and predestination. According to Finney, Christ had died to remove the blemish of original sin from man's soul, but his death did not ensure salvation to all. With Christ's death, God proclaimed "a universal amnesty inviting all men to repent, to believe in Christ, and to accept salvation." All were free to accept salvation, but those who turned away would be justly punished.[11]

Finney is central to our concerns because his new theology opened the door for the acceptance of Perfectionism as a legitimate religious doctrine. Contrary to Calvinist orthodoxy and the thought of Jonathan Edwards, man was not born morally corrupt and depraved. It was ignorance and self-interest that bound man to an unregenerate state. Winning his soul for God meant first riveting his attention and then reorienting his personality. The task of the preacher was to create an existential shock in the heart and mind of the unregenerate, to jar him or her out of spiritual complacency or predisposition to sin. Wickedness was the choice of men and converting them meant helping them grasp the alternative. Edwards could only exhort his listeners to open their hearts and hope for the miraculous intervention of God. Finney was the engineer of conversion, drawing a blueprint to guide a person's freely willed regeneration. For miraculous intervention, he substituted systematic, self-conscious techniques to ignite the spirit—preacher and Holy Spirit worked as a team.

The evangelists of the second Great Awakening made American Protestantism more harmonious with the democratic ideal than it had been before. The patient waiting on God counseled by Edwards could be disappointing if one was not among the predetermined elect. Systematic application of Finneyite "new measures" universalized salvation and was more in tune with the democratic doctrine of the free individual. The restraint of evil in the individual and society had been a central feature of Calvinism, but with the fall of the doctrine of fundamental human depravity, evangelical religion came even closer to the theory of American constitutionalism.

Revivals employing Finneyite "new measures" were frantic affairs involving all-night prayer meetings; praying for sinners by name; allowing women to pray and exhort in the presence of men; denouncing "old school" ministers as cold, stupid, or dead; employing an "anxious seat" or bench at the front of the assembly to which awakening sinners were called for special prayers and exhortation; and informal, spontaneous, vernacular sermons that appealed to the heart rather than the head.

Finney took the West by storm but was opposed in the East by the formidable Lyman Beecher. Fearing that the fanaticism, excess emotionalism, hysteria, and disorder of the "new measures" would tarnish the reputation of revivalism, Beecher proposed a convention at New Lebanon, New York, for July 1827 to iron out ministerial and theological disputes. When Finney accepted the invitation, Beecher took it as a sign that he would finally come around and listen to reason. At the end of the convention, neither side could claim it had converted the other. Finney agreed to discourage "audible groaning, boisterous shouting, fainting, and other convulsions where possible," but remained adamant to any further compromise. Beecher and his followers were equally tenacious in their own beliefs. If either side profited from the convention, it was the Finneyites, for it provided a well-publicized forum for their views. Ultimately, Beecher's public opposition to the "new measures" softened—though not his private distaste—as Finneyites met with greater success and popularity in the East, including Beecher's own Boston stronghold. By 1840 the evangelical views of Finney, and the more moderate ones of Beecher and Nathaniel Taylor, had penetrated every nonliturgical congregation save the Old School Presbyterians and Baptists.

Revivalism preaching an activist ethic triggered personal conversions and attempts to regenerate society at large. John L. Hammond has suggested that the collective experience of revival strengthened the motivation to act on the beliefs preached. As a life-changing event, it provided a general orientation to social and political activism channeled in particular areas and utilizing particular methods. The revivalist calling to benevolence was both explicit and specific, spawning antislavery and abolition societies, temperance and Sabbath-keeping movements, numerous tract and missionary societies, and many other philanthropic organizations. The antislavery movement was especially important in that its religious base—the ideas that all men are equal before God and that slavery is inconsistent with the doctrine of free will—provided a forum for the dissemination of democratic ideals. The revivalist conviction that sin, be it personal or societal, required vigorous opposition was expressed in the formation of political parties that championed antislavery or abolitionism in the 1830s and 1840s.[12]

Alongside the democratic and radical proclivities of some revivalists stood the contrasting tendencies of a strong conservative wing. Beecher began as a progressive, favoring equality, removal of privilege, and the regulation of economic activity, and he showed an interest in the plight of the workingman. In the 1830s, Beecher began his drift toward conservatism, partly because of his distrust of radicals such as Fanny Wright and Robert Dale Owens. He condemned the Workingmen's Party—organized by Wright, Owens, and other free-thinking intellectuals in 1829—as an "infidel trumpet-call to all the envious and vicious poor."[13]

The second Great Awakening also stirred another, more radical political current, Antimasonry, which not only tapped evangelical Protestantism's democratic vein, but also directly confronted the nondemocratic features of society and polity.

Antimasonry: The Democratic Ideal Fed with Religious Intensity

Antimasonry, a movement and later a political party, emerged in 1826 from the mysterious disappearance and suspected murder of William Morgan, a "renegade" from the Masonic order who had written a book purporting to reveal its secrets.[14] Morgan was never seen again, but David Miller, the Batavia printer who published his revelation, had not been silenced. He struck back at his Masonic persecutors, publishing a lengthy account of Morgan's abduction. Filled with lurid speculation and impassioned rhetoric, Miller called on the public to demand Masonic criminals be brought to justice.

As time passed and Morgan's disappearance remained a mystery, the thrust of the issue shifted from the fate of one man to the question of whether there existed a secret society powerful enough to establish a system of private justice and to thwart official attempts at investigation and punishment. The cry of conspiracy arose when local committees failed to move state and local organs of government to take what they considered appropriate action in connection with Morgan's kidnapping. The question became whether any secret society was compatible with republican institutions.

By becoming a political party Antimasonry pushed democratic ideology to its Rousseauian limits, for it insisted that no restrictions should be placed on the will of the people. Where Rousseau had doubts about how it was possible to ascertain the "general will" as the standard of morality, the Antimasons had no such reservations: public opinion must govern everything. The masses were mobilized and polarized by the issue.

Evangelical churches were expanding rapidly in the area and they embraced Antimasonry enthusiastically. It was felt that Masonry had come to serve many in place of the church. Its oath took the Lord's name in vain, and, at the very least, it interposed a prior association among certain church members who were bound equally with all regenerate souls. Rumors that alcoholic beverages were used with abandon in its ceremonies irritated a growing temperance sensibility. Its titles and rituals smacked of monarchy as well as infidelity, and its very secrecy suggested ignoble and dangerous designs.

Antimasonry extended egalitarian doctrines to embrace all aspects of American life and invested the egalitarian impulse with religious intensity and legitimacy. Claiming Freemasonry exerted a dangerous influence on Christian people, the Antimasonic party was viewed by many as a "Christian party" in politics. All aspects of American politics became grist for the Antimasonic political mills. "Impurities" in America could and must be removed by the electoral process.

Although the second Great Awakening did contain an intolerant, dictatorial, moral dualism, its exaggerated concern for the individual provided its democratic thrust. In theory, complete equality dwelt among the regenerate and the benevolent movements aimed at converting every last sinner, but these movements' exclusive concern with the state of the individual soul turned their attention from direct confrontation with political and economic institutions. The antislavery movement is a notable exception, but its basic thrust was moral rather than democratic idealism. Evangelical revivalism's theory of social change was contingent upon prior spiritual regeneration. The good and just social order could only emerge out of a regenerate nation. The popular and fiery preachers of the second Great Awakening did perfect an intensely emotional and vernacular religious style that was congenial to the common man and in stark contrast to the religious establishment run by and for the privileged class.

Aristocracy and Inequality in New York State: The Tension
between Religious and Democratic Ideals and Political Life

We have seen the ideological consonance between nineteenth-century American Protestantism and the democratic ideal, but democracy had yet to achieve universal approval.[15]

The "French philosophy"—associated with Jacobinism in the North—was widely feared by the Federalists who were partisans of England, the source of their wealth. To be a Federalist meant embracing the political philosophy of Edmund Burke and refusing to tamper with the traditional ways in which wealth was represented.

At the turn of the nineteenth century, New York State was not without its aristocracy. This aristocracy was mostly Dutch rather than Puritan, but it appealed to Puritan sensibilities on the questions of wealth and real estate. William Bayard, the Bleekers, C. D. Coldern, James Ematt, and Nicholas Fish were all prominent Federalists holding large tracts of land by grant or purchase from the state. Alexander Hamilton, the Roosevelts, James Watson, Josiah Ogden Hoffman, Frederic De Peyster, Garret Van Horne, Stephen Van Rensselaer, Philip Schuyler, and Gouverneur Morris were all large landowners and men of wealth and influence in the Federalist party. All were as keenly interested in the politics of land as in that of trade, banks, or industrial securities.

While many made their way into the wilderness to be rid of every vestige of feudalism, the Ogdens, the Rensselaers, and others came to reproduce the aristocratic tradition. The open reaches of northern New York State provided the ideal setting for a manorial life-style of equestrian outings, lordship over a docile tenantry, and aristocratic politics. The influence of this "squirearchy" was conservative, looking backward to the Tory model across the Atlantic. They were patrons of "the Episcopal mode of worship, so friendly to Government, so hostile to Jacobinism."[16] This conservative influence was distributed throughout the counties of the state, which somewhat checked the spirit of democracy.

Despite similarities in philosophical outlook and the absence of ideological conflict between the established families and the bulk of the populace, there was a deep-seated resentment of the aristocracy by a large portion of the people. During the Revolution many of the patroons were stripped of their baronial powers, and lost some of their special legal privileges and feudal rights such as entail and primogeniture. Tory holdings had been confiscated, bought up by speculators, and in many cases sold in small lots to farming families. The antirent movement, triggered by the devastating effects of the death of Stephen Van Rensselaer III and the provision of his will that creditors be paid with rent arrears (estimated at $400,000), gained popular support and spread to other estates. The movement, courted by John Yound, the Whig candidate and winner of the governor's seat in 1846, crystallized into a block vote. Sensing popular sentiment against them and fearing court mandated divesture, the members of the squirearchy began selling their holdings before their very titles could be questioned (as, in fact, they were).

With the beginning of the assault on the family aristocracies, another external indicator of status disappeared. Politics and the pursuit of political office became more important than ever as avenues of social ascension. The decline of the Hudson Valley squirearchy, though significant, did not eliminate the aristocratic influence in New York. As the countryside became less aristocratic, a New York City–centered commercial, industrial, and financial plutocracy took root in the fertile laissez-faire economy.

Certainly the New York State aristocracy was opposed to the absolute political equality of citizens, but that class also represented a social theory that opposed the growing democratic thrust of American Protestantism. Burgeoning evangelicism recognized no source of religious status except conversion and spiritual regeneration. A noble family line, large estate, or aristocratic tastes and life-style neither marked God's grace nor eased one's conversion. In fact, the concerns of maintaining and expanding family wealth, and especially aristocratic consumption, smacked of a greed, worldliness, and irresponsibility that stemmed from neglecting the stewardship of wealth. The priority of selfish and material concerns would make the aristocrat a less-likely candidate for salvation. The religious virtue of the comman man lay in his democratic lack of spiritual and social pretensions.

New York State Politics and the Religious Undercurrent of Democratic Reform

Ideology played a virtually nonexistent role in New York politics during the early nineteenth century. The political arena can be characterized as an essentially one-party system of Republicans (including Clintonians and Bucktails) and a marginal, isolated Federalist party (associated with Toryism, British influence, and aristocracy).

The lack of any ideological dispute is well demonstrated by the defection of many Federalists to the Republican side in their pursuit of public office.

New York's political parties during the pre-Jacksonian period were highly personalized machines organized for the conquest of political and administrative office. All significant factions centered around notable personalities such as George Clinton, Aaron Burr, Morgan Lewis, Daniel D. Tompkins, De Witt Clinton, and Martin Van Buren. Inextricably tied to leading personalities and possessing a somewhat seasonal character, factions and leadership in state-wide politics tended to be ephemeral. New parties, factions, and leaders continually emerged, rose to power, shifted alliances, and disappeared as others took their place. With prestige and patronage as the prizes, political leaders were not obstructed by principle in their shifting alliances. Practical considerations, uncontaminated by ideology and principle, almost always determined the side taken on a particular issue.[17]

Discipline was imposed through a patronage system that assured the concentration of power and privilege in the hands of a wealthy elite stratum with little input from below. This spoils system was served by its associated appendages: the party press, fellowship societies, government institutions like the Council of Revision, the Council of Appointment, and the Congressional caucus, and the indirect choice of presidential electors by the state legislature.

The structure and orientation of political parties, the absence of ideological dialogue and conflict, and the commitment of parties and politicians to opportunism and the spoils system brought into question the moral foundations of politics. A politics based upon careerism, spoils, and expediency—and the resultant corruption and self-seeking—flew in the face of a Calvinist legacy that insisted upon the restraint of evil in the individual and government. Revivalism, Antimasonry, and the call for a Christian party in politics—though differing over several points on the relationship between religion and politics—converged on a fundamental theme: the moral and religious excellence of the regenerate Christian was the source of the common man's political competence. A democratic politics, overwhelming the personal political machines by extending suffrage and the direct election of officials, would open the government to the influence of the regenerate. The moral degeneracy of both state and civil society could be reversed by extending the influence of a democratic, evangelical Protestantism to the political sphere.

The initial institutional impulse to democratize the state political system came from a faction committed to the status quo but temporarily out of favor and office. It was primarily through the efforts of the Clintonians that the state convention in 1817 supplanted the legislative caucus as a method of nominating gubernatorial candidates. The manner in which the state nominating convention was introduced provides the pattern for most of the other democratic innovations that followed in subsequent years. Opportunistic politicians without any permanent or recognizably consistent commitments pushed democratic causes that they felt would promote their own ambitions. The "democratic banner" moved back and forth among different factions, depending on particular circumstances and the political plums at stake.

The total body of political maneuvers and debates that finally institutionalized many of the democratic reforms in New York State are too lengthy to discuss in light of the subject at hand, although a few words must be said concerning two central issues resolved by the convention: that of suffrage and of the Council of Appointments.

Suffrage elicited the greatest debates of the convention. Religion and theology did not take a prominent place in the debates but they formed the ideological foundation for democratic reform. "There were those to whom democracy was something more than a form of government—a destiny of perfection, indeed, proceeding 'as uniformly and majestically as the laws of being and as certain as the decrees of eternity.' "[18] This democratic sentiment recalled the fundamental harmonies between American Protestantism and the democratic ideal. Spiritual and political perfection joined with progressive optimism and it was anticipated that the laws of the political order would reflect the God-given moral law. The question of suffrage and the direct election of officials revolved around a related religious theme, the moral qualities of the common man; and Protestant universalism and evangelical confidence in the masses were reflected in the debate over the issue. Federalists and conservatives argued that political responsibility grew out of a vested interest in the political and economic order. Democratic reformers and their affiliated party press stressed the honesty and moral dignity of the working man and the working poor who had built and patronized America's civic and religious institutions. It was their God-given right to have their political voice be heard.[19]

The committee on suffrage reported for a liberal extension: every white male citizen twenty-one years old or older, residing for six months within his district and paying taxes, or who, on assessment, had performed some work upon the public roads or had been enrolled in the militia, might vote for any office elected by the people. The opposition spoke of an "apparent disposition to vibrate from a well-balanced government to the extremes of democratic doctrines. ... Such a proposition as that contained in the report, at the distance of ten years past, would have struck the public mind with astonishment and terror."[20] Fundamentally, the debate centered around the values of property versus people, and the franchise tied to property was the Federalists's strongest link in their chain of defense.

After much haggling, the committee brought in a proposal very similar to that which had been originally offered. It was fought clause by clause, but the resolution finally carried by a margin of nearly two to one. Conservatives hoped that some privilege might be preserved by a requirement that a candidate for senator must have $1,000 worth of real estate, but even this was denied. A simple free-holder was declared eligible for office and the external constraints on the moral individual had been lifted.

The Council of Appointments, a long-coveted source of patronage and privilege, was also on the agenda and ultimately was abolished. The committee on the subject recommended that civil servants be elected and that militia officers, except the very highest, be elected by the men-in-arms. Several high offices of the state administration, such as the treasurer, comptroller, and secretary of state, were now to be selected by the legislature, while others were to be appointed by the governor and confirmed by the senate.

After 1821 there was no question about the theory of government acceptable to New York State. The triumphant democrats set out to purge the state of all practices reminiscent of aristocracy, privilege, and royalty. The vanquished Federalists had exhausted their ammunition with little result except to intensify the prejudice against them. Some were never reconciled, but most old-party men joined with other followers of Clinton as if they were in full accord with the new theory. For the next few years factions contended to prove themselves more friendly to the people than their rivals. "In the arsenal of journalistic epithets, the word 'aristocrat' was thought the deadliest of all. ..."[21] Although the Federalists ceased to be a viable political party, Federalism as a political philosophy did not die out immediately. Democratic leaders continued to fear Federalists bearing votes and were resolved not to share their patronage.

This brief summary of political trends and events of the early nineteenth century was intended to point out the tension between Protestantism and the romantic notions of democracy, and the realpolitik of politicians, political machines, and governmental institutions that, while consistently paying lip service to democratic ideals, was tempered by an acute fear of the masses. Except for Antimasonry and the antislavery and abolition movement, revival religion shied away from direct confrontation with political institutions. Revivalists railed at the moral and political corruption of elected and appointed state officials but, for the most part, they called for individual conversion: regenerate officials were counted on to set the political system on a moral foundation. Beneath the political debate flowed a theological undercurrent. The doctrines of a God-given moral law, moral politics, political perfectionism, and progress, and the free individual and the moral and political competence of the common man were the Protestant legacy that resonated in New York State's democratic reforms.

Democratic Theocracy: The Political Thought of John Humphrey Noyes

None of the major religious voices of the day was able to overcome the conflict between religion and democracy or the conflict within religion over democracy. The political influence of revival Protestantism did not go far enough to suit John Humphrey Noyes. Sacred utopia required more than an injection of religion into the political system: religion and democracy had to be merged. The kingdom of God was not democratic; it was to be a divine monarchy based upon inspiration and immutable moral law. In short, Noyes sought to reestablish the "democracy" of the Puritan commonwealth's town meeting. Debate, divisiveness, and conflict should only go as far as determining where inspiration lay. Once religious principles and inspiration were ascertained, consensus was ethically and empirically expected. Democracy was clearly the highest form of civil administration, but it was only a transitional form between monarchical and despotic government and the kingdom of God. The democracy of regenerate souls had to be combined with the elitism of religious virtuosos who were most capable of ascertaining God's will. This was the core of democratic theocracy.

The evening meeting and mutual criticism were the organizational forums in which democratic theocracy was elaborated at the Oneida Community. Evening meetings were partly social and partly religious gatherings. Everyday community affairs, religious issues, and the thoughts of John Humphrey Noyes were discussed. The meeting was also the communal decision-making body. A wide variety of economic, social, and religious issues were discussed, debated, and balloted. If serious opposition to any question persisted, the issue was tabled and worked over until consensus was achieved, or it was dropped if unanimity was impossible. Noyes, as God's representative and the architect of the kingdom of heaven on earth, could be counted upon for inspiration, insight into God's will, and forging consensus.

Mutual criticism gave further opportunity for the democracy of regenerate souls to express itself in social control. From time to time, each community member was expected to submit to spiritual criticism, praise, and evaluation by a committee of peers who would make suggestions for a program of improvement. Effective criticism was considered an art that each member was obligated to develop and practice.

We shall see in later chapters that the transcendence of the tension between religion and democracy in democratic theocracy was viable only as long as agreement on fundamental religious principles could be counted on. Once the religious unity of the community began to show signs of erosion the democratic aspects of Oneida life and politics developed into conflict and factionalism, and inspiration was no longer strong enough to maintain solidarity and commitment.

We have seen that American Protestantism, from Puritanism through the second Great Awakening, contained contradictory thoughts and sentiments concerning democracy. On the one hand we found four significant parallels between democratic and Protestant ideals. First, the doctrine of a fundamental moral law was common to the American democratic faith and the law of the Divine Monarch; second, Calvin's insistence on the restraint of evil in both individual and government resonated with American constitutionalism; third, the doctrines of free will and the equality of regenerate souls provided a theological basis for revivalism and political reform; and fourth, the utopian vision of American ideals and institutions was represented as the leading edge of secular progress, the potential savior of the autocratic Old World, and a secular version of the Christian millennial mission.

On the other hand, we also found in Puritanism a tendency toward moral absolutism, spiritual intolerance, and a vehement insistence of harmony and consensus in religious and political matters that flew in the face of democratic forms. In revivalism we likewise found persistent tensions between religion and democracy. Alongside the strong democratic and radical sentiments of many second Great Awakening preachers was a conservative revivalist wing apprehensive over the "new measures," distrustful of the religious and political proclivities of the masses, and in principled theological opposition to tampering with the political and economic status quo.

In the political arena we saw the tension between Protestant and secular democratic ideologies and the political order, and we saw the role of religious ideas in New York's democratic reform movement.

Thus we have located two kinds of tension between religion and democracy: tensions within the religious sphere, and tensions between religion and the secular political order. John Humphrey Noyes was dissatisfied with the partial resolutions offered by revivalism and secular political reform, and chose, instead, to reach for a transcendent utopian solution—democratic theocracy—that would merge the needs of democratic social control and administration with theocratic authority.

4
The Tension between
Religion and Sex,
Women, and
the Family

For John Humphrey Noyes, an essential step in the progressive redemption of humanity was the transcendence of monogamous sex and marriage and the adoption of a system in which men and women loved one another collectively rather than in pairs. Sex was to be elevated to the level of a sacrament through which the individual absorbed spiritual energy in a communion with God and one's partner. Collective sexual life also offered the opportunity for scientific breeding of more spiritually and intellectually advanced offspring and reproduction of the community itself. Noyes's sexual theory was at the core of his program for spiritual perfection and, as we shall see, reverberated in all spheres of the Oneida Community's life.

Within the Judeo-Christian tradition, sex was transformed from an instinct and appetite to a matter of right and wrong. This transvaluation may be considered the consequence of a triple alienation: the alienation from God, from the body, and from the social collectivity. Of course, Christianity has not regarded all sexual behavior as sinful, but the dichotomy between acceptable sexual practice and lust provides a focal point for examining Christianity's ambivalence toward sex. It is neither advisable nor advantageous to examine what produces and directs the tension between sex and religion on a philosophical or ethical plane alone. Its impulses must be found in the "facts of life" of man's social existence and conditions.

Pagan cultures long celebrated fertility rites, venerated the earth mother and phallic symbols, but the Judeo-Christian tradition alienated sex from religion with the notion of "original sin." That primal failing transformed naturalness to nakedness and the coordinate awareness of sexual desire became sinful. In theological terms, sexuality is a consequence of man's alienation from God.

For St. Augustine, the original sin snatched procreation and sex from man's will.[1] No longer could man effectively exert control over his sexual organs or desires. Sexual passions and activities became perfidious peformances not subject to reason or total social control. Not only is man alienated from his God, he is disjoined from his body as well. The sexual organs and desires are no longer simply the means of procreation and for God's glory; they are also the agents of lust and demonic forces.

The sinfulness of lust cannot be solely derived from man's alienation from God and his own body. It also suggests a "jealous" social order. Lest one's passion and paramour absorb all interests, activities, and energies and promote an asocial neglect of other values and obligations, "societies with quite diverse cultures have sought to weaken the opportunities and inhibit the passions that lead to such departure and duty."[2]

Man's divorce from God and the control of his body provided the theological underpinning to the tension between religion and the erotic sphere, but our central concern will be the expression of this tension in the sociocultural aspects of life in nineteenth-century America. Unfortunately, folkways, mores, and taboos of sexual life for the common man in pre-twentieth-century America remain out of reach to the historian. Milton Rugoff notes that even those inclined to diary- and journal-keeping are exceptionally circumspect and reserved in this regard. We are left with the occasional writings of the upper classes, such as Benjamin Franklin's "Advice to a Young Man on Choosing a Mistress," the diatribes of radicals such as William Godwin, Mary Wollstonecraft, Robert Dale Owens, and Francis Wright; marriage and etiquette manuals; and medical/moral tracts bent on establishing a "Victorian" sexual ideology.[3] In spite of the risk of distortion, these sources expose the tension between religion and sexuality, and the contested place of sexuality in American life.

The Tension between Sex and Religion: Puritanism's Sexual Ambivalence

Sexual frigidity, repression of sensuous enjoyment, and the prudish avoidance of biological facts had not been a part of Martin Luther's makeup nor were they inherent in Protestantism at its origin. It appeared only among the extremist factions of those who followed Luther. Luther himself had married and had evidently found the sexual side of marriage satisfactory.[4] He argued that sexual love was as natural and necessary as other biological requirements. Calvin retained the medieval idea that sex was sinful, but within marriage the natural impulse was sanctified and left untainted. Although keeping to a natural notion of sex, mediated by its innate sinfulness, Luther was hardly ecstatic over the role of sex in the world, as can be surmised from this remark: "Had God consulted me about it I should have advised Him to continue the generation of the species by fashioning human beings out of clay, as Adam was made."[5]

Later, Calvin drew together the most severe elements of the Old Testament, patristic writings, and Lutheranism, and derived a ferocious theology built upon depravity, the implacable wrath of God, and predestination with election for the few and damnation for the rest. Taking the post of head of the Geneva Consistory (the religious government of Geneva) Calvin assumed dictatorial control over morality. His view on sex, love, and other pleasures of life became the code under which Genevans would live for the next century.

Calvin likened conjugal relations to that existing between Christ and the believer, insisting on fidelity in marriage and religion. But marriage itself was simply a last resort, a vent to passion when self-control failed. Singing, dancing at weddings, swearing, extravagant clothing, and too many courses at dinner could be punished by fine or imprisonment. Plays were banned, jewelry and other items of personal adornment discouraged, and elegant hair styles were reason for internment. Sexual transgressions drew as severe a punishment as heresy: fornication merited exile, adultery deserved death. Some Genevans were punished in these ways, although many sexual offenders were excused with steep fines and jail sentences.

In Puritan sexuality we observe the first expression of what was to be a continuing tension between sex and American Protestantism: throughout American history, sex has swung on a moral pendulum of religious approval and anxiety. Puritanism was heir to a stern, sober, supramorality, but its historical portrayal has tended more toward caricature than accuracy. For all their emphasis on the sinfulness of fornication and adultery, the early Puritans were not against sex as such, only against sex outside marriage. They raised—and took pride in—large families and praised married sex while condemning the papal virginal ideal, but insisted that sex must not interfere with man's duty to God or cause him to neglect his religious obligations. Puritanism's inner-worldly orientation and its religious obligations governing reproduction and harmonious family life fostered a recognition of sexuality as an essential human trait, and a means of fulfilling one's duty to God and community. But sex also had the potential for alienating man from God and his religious and civic duties by catering to individual hedonistic gratification opposed to the spiritual and communal values that contributed to God's glory and the Puritan commonwealth.[6]

In spite of the caricatures of Puritan life, which are more "puritanical" than Puritan, and the contrary depictions of Puritans as "simultaneously frank, strongly sexed, and somewhat romantic,"[7] there is no need to opt for one or the other picture. The Puritans were of two minds concerning their sexuality, drawn by a sensual siren and constrained by conscience.[8] This inner conflict, rendered individually inexpressible by Protestant propriety, could only be vented by congregational morality plays (in which members were tried for sexual and marital offenses) and, in the early nineteenth century, by ecclesiastical councils.

The public confession of fornication before marriage was not compelled by the potential for embarrassment if the congregation discovered the offense, but was rooted in fear of infant damnation. The records of a Groton, Connecticut, church suggest that confessions to premarital sex were more than just occasional churchly entertainments. Of the 200 persons bound in baptism from 1761–1775, no less than 66 publicly confessed to sex before marriage. Nine of the sixteen couples admitted to full communion between 1789–1791 similarly "confessed." In Braintree, Massachusetts, there seemed to be a marked increase in public confessions during the first Great Awakening.[9] The connection between sexual and religious excitement was not missed by William I. Thomas, who observed that the appeal made to the unconverted during a religious revival has some psychological resemblance to the male attempt to overcome female hesitancy. In each case the will must be set aside, and, to accomplish this, strong suggestive means and appeals of the pleading, sympathetic, and intimate type are used.[10] In fact, revivalist preachers were often suspected of taking advantage of newly repentant women, and were for this reason the butt of slanderous rumor. In marked contrast to communal titillation by public confession was the attempt to suppress stimulation in social amusements. The Puritans attacked the vernal Maypole and condemned and punished "charmers," seducers, seductresses, and their victims.

Thus American Protestantism maintained sex and religion in a chronic state of tension. On the one hand Puritans suspected the innate sinfulness of sex, saw the temptations of the flesh as trials of ascetic self-control, and feared that licentiousness led to neglect of religious duties. On the other hand, religious caution did not lead to a significant degree of abstemiousness, for the Puritans had a clear sympathy for romantic love and human sexual needs, and understood their importance in family and community harmony.

American Victorianism, Revivalism, and the Tension between Sex and Religion

American Victorianism, like the English original, was in some respects propelled by the desire for stability in a rapidly changing social and economic environment. Victorianism not only tried to put the collective house in order, embarking on political reform, Sunday schools, hospitals, and other benevolent activities, but it also tried to stabilize private life through an exaggerated worship of domestic home life and romantic love. The home was more than shelter, it was a refuge from the commercial world where men could be reassured that they still possessed warm emotions and human feelings.

Urbanization, industrialization, and the perceived stretching of morality that seemed to accompany the advance of the frontier appeared, to many, to be rapidly eroding man's moral fiber. Worshiping domesticity and the creed of the ideal woman was only one "Victorian" response; albeit one that had severe repercussions for sexuality in general, and the perception of female sexuality in particular. Although the term "Victorian" has been associated with sexual repression, neurosis, and pathology, recent studies dismiss these characterizations as extrapolations from myth and an ideology-seeking establishment rather than a reflection of actual behavior. Carl Degler notes that this distortion of the Victorian era is partly the result of social historians overlooking or ignoring the literature that did not reflect exaggerated prudery.[11] The usual literature cited—ranging from academic monographs, marriage manuals, guides to midwifery and domestic medicine, to outright quackery—portrays "normal" women as having little or no appetite for or enjoyment of sex, and it validated the "double standard" on physiological grounds. That a large body of literature existed questioning these notions suggests that the literature of prudery did not reflect actual attitudes or practices, and, more important for our concerns, that there was a high degree of heretofore unnoticed ideological conflict over sexuality.

The rise of an ideology of sexual repression has been associated with the emergence of a dominant middle class in America. Self-denial, control, and predictability permeated the middle-class economic and social ethic. Licentiousness, uncontrolled sexuality, and promiscuity were associated with the lower classes, and it was these moral weaknesses that accounted for their low rank. Servants, as the representatives of the lower class in the middle-class home, were especially suspect. Popular literature frequently warned the lady of the house to beware of the corrupting unseemly affections and influences that servants might exert on the young members of the household. Repressed sexuality, warnings of masturbatory "drain," self-control, and the deferment of sexual satisfaction were parts of the emotional currents that ran parallel to an economic ethos encouraging saving, investment, vitality, production, and success. The legacy of Puritan inner-worldly asceticism was reflected in its sexual economy.

In addition to this economic explanation, Charles E. Rosenberg introduces a more intriguing line of thought. In the eighteenth and early nineteenth century, indictments of "sexual excess" were routine yet calm and bland in tone. Sexual activity after puberty was accepted as both natural and necessary. The trend toward sexual repressiveness correlates with the active millennialism of the generation following the second Great Awakening. Beginning with the 1830s the spokespersons for sexual repression took on a more strident tone. For some, sexuality acquired an absolutely negative cast. The Shakers, Rappites, Zoarites, and the Ephrata Community all repudiated sex as incompatible with a pure Christian life.[12] "Excessive" sexual activity threatened women with uterine infection, hysteria, irregular menstruation, and barrenness. Men were susceptible to physical "drain," debility, weakness, impotence, back problems, and a predisposition to innumerable diseases.

Control was the building block of sound stature and personality. Allowing the passions free play would destroy any chance of establishing the calm equilibrium of mind and body necessary to the

Christian personality. As evangelical preachers assailed the passions and ways of the flesh as sinful and polluting, as distractions from piety and as temptations from the underworld, and extolled the ideal of the "Christian gentleman," their sermons clashed with the archaic male ethos that applauded the physical vigor, aggressiveness, and sexual athletics of the male achiever. Women were caught in no less conflict of sexual role as the ideal of female purity and passivity confronted the ideal mother/wife as nurturer. True nurturance implied sexual warmth and availability. Excessive sexual repression was one of the results of these role conflicts.

American Victorianism and evangelical religion tapped into the middle-class and ascetic Protestant celebration of discipline, self-control, and propriety as the ideals of worldly ethics. The sober, righteous, and regenerate "Christian gentleman," and the domestic, pure, and angelic female were the highest expression of this evangelical-Victorian ethos. But alongside this sexual repressiveness stood a significant medical, scientific, and popular literature and sentiment that recognized sexual pleasure and gratification as natural, normal, and intrinsically human.

Religion, Sex, and Asociality

From Puritanism to the second Great Awakening we have seen a Protestant and middle-class ideology that has condemned sexual "excess"—and sometimes sex altogether—as an iniquitous drain on and diversion from the social collectivity. Most of the material in this vein is psychohistorical. When we turn to the ecclesiastical councils and trials of New England, we find explicit, direct evidence of the link between sexual sinfulness and asociality. The ecclesiastical council of Rupert, Vermont, trying a case of seduction, clearly shows how firmly intertwined were the religious and social questions pertaining to seduction and fornication.[13]

If the seducer was able to marry his victim—if he was not himself married or betrothed—argued the council, he was obliged to, for several reasons. First, the marriage would clearly be for his own good since the guilt he had acquired rendered him unfit to marry another. He would be subject to painful reflections and, of course, the reproach of others. Second, he had no other way to make reparation to the woman. He had drawn her into a sin against God, destroyed her character, and deprived her of the privilege of marrying another. Third, *the interests of society* require he marry the one he had se-

duced. Seducers, once their reputations are known, will rarely have
the opportunity to marry. They will be disinclined to marry, their
sense of honor will be extinguished, and their "wild and roving"
libidinous desires will prevail. The natural consequences of such a
state are "insubordination, contempt for the institution of marriage,
deception of every kind, intemperate drinking, loathsome diseases,
spurious progeny, "murderous artifices to prevent propagation,
subversion of government and social happiness," and the "introduction of complete wretchedness."

Fornication provides justifiable pretext for divorce "not because it
is the greatest sin that can be committed; nor because it tends more,
than any other, to interrupt domestic happiness; but because it im-
plies the fraud of contract." Not only does it violate the law of God,
it tears asunder the fundamental institutions of social order: marriage and the contract.[14]

Evangelical Christians preached and manifested an equally repressive sexual ideology threatening eternal damnation for lustful actions and thoughts, and warning of dire social decay if they were not
controlled. The Shakers and other like-minded sects confronted the
sexual threat to piety and collectivity by opting for celibacy. The
Oneida Community melded economic and familial systems: a communism of economy and sexual/familial affection in which devotion
to God and community was expressed in full spiritual and sexual
love.

Women's Roles and the Tension between Religion and World

Christian misogyny began with the Pauline idea that God com-
manded women to be subject to men as punishment for the temptation of Adam and the introduction of sin into the world. Furthermore, Adam was created in God's image and Eve from man's rib,
almost as an afterthought. The cult of celibacy, the virgin, and monasticism, insists Barbara J. Harris, was based upon the assumption
that woman is the temptress, man the tempted. Monasticism was not
a response to a secularized Christianity, as many have argued, but
rather a flight from woman.[15]

It was not until the Renaissance that misogynous ideas began to be
questioned, but humanist ideas about the education of women were
stunted by the Protestant Reformation's Pauline-derived theology.
The European Protestant legacy imported to English North America
thus included traditional ideas on the inferiority and subjugation of

women and at the same time newer Reformation attitudes toward women's education, universal literacy and responsibility for interpreting Scripture, the rejection of the celibate ideal, and the duty to marry. Milton's *Paradise Lost*, a favorite of pious Puritans, summed up their cultural and religious philosophy in regard to the relation between the sexes:

... Both
Not equal, as their sex not equal, seemed;
For contemplation he and valor formed,
For softness she and sweet attractive grace;
He for God only, she for God in him.
His fair large front and eye sublime declared
Absolute rule. . . .[16]

Religious ideals provided the moral and normative framework for women's role, but Puritan pragmatism also accepted worldly demands as an essential part of the Puritan religious condition. The strenuous demands of the New World never permitted the realization of Milton's Edenic ideal. The environment insisted on strong, self-reliant women with the ability to shoulder responsibility rather than "softness . . . and sweet attractive grace." In practice, the frontier altered women's roles, but nonetheless maintained the boundaries, the ideal, and patriarchal authority, though it softened the inherited notion of absolute male dominance.

From the seed of ideal feminine virtue sprouted woman's separate sphere and the cult of true womanhood. The cardinal virtues of piety, purity, submissiveness, and domesticity permeated the popular literature, especially women's magazines, of the nineteenth century. Manifesting these virtues, women were the protectors of morals, religion, and the household. Pure in heart and mind, the ideal woman of the nineteenth century was just short of angelic.[17]

Despite reduced birth and mortality rates, growing population concentration, decline of home manufacturing, economic mobility, later marriage, and less time spent procuring food and clothing—all drastic changes in the life of women—the cult of true womanhood and ideal femininity remained rigid. The ideal woman was expected to be emotional, feminine, and gentle, but social conditions and the notion of the ideal mother demanded strong, self-reliant, protective, and efficient managers of children and home.

The disjunction between the feminine ideal and the demands of the everyday life of women was not the only contradiction; the ideal itself carried the seeds of its own destruction. Women were regarded as the moral protectors of society but were excluded from activities that would have brought their "angelic" nature to bear on a corrupt world.[18] If this line had been advanced only by secular and radical feminists, the women's movement would have been significantly held back. The democratic impulse of the second Great Awakening and its benevolent ethos tapped this tension within Protestantism— the legacy of Christian misogyny countered by the purity and piety of woman—and the dichotomy of corrupt society and the moral sanctuary of the herth. We must remember, though, that the vast majority of revivalist preachers and leaders were not radical feminists in principle; they only sought to use the moral and religious force of women as a means of transcending the tension between religious ideals and secular corruption. They did not attempt to break down sex role boundaries, but only to use the moral authority of women in wider society.

The second Great Awakening significantly elevated the status of women in religious life, in that they became involved in virtually all its aspects. Women were terribly important to revivalists because they seemed so much more receptive to the emotionalism of the "new measures," and provided a foothold at the very foundation of the family. Women now prayed and exhorted with men and were granted full participation in revivals. They were even more prominent in smaller prayer groups and Bible classes. As revival asceticism compelled the converted to overcome the sinfulness in individuals and society at large, women figured prominently in missionary and tracts associations and in benevolent societies concerned with slavery, moral reform, education, and temperance.

While enthusiastic religion extended woman's sphere to the moral reform of the world, legal reform lagged. Even at mid-century, women had no legally recognized individuality. On marriage a husband became the legal head of the household with power over property. A wife could not sue alone, execute a deed, or bind herself and property in contract. Control over personal property was forfeited for as long as the marriage lasted. Not until 1860 did the New York State legislature grant married women possession of their own wages and equal guardianship over their children. During the Civil War these newly granted rights were taken away from widows. In short, women were considered chattel, transferable to a man upon marriage.[19]

Women could refuse to marry, but that was a costly decision. Upon the death of their parents, unwed daughters lived with married relatives as virtually wageless household menials. To be a wage earner meant exclusion from neighborhood functions, and it was believed that any woman who voluntarily sought a vocation outside of domestic service was unfit to be a wife and mother.

Once again, the conservative nature of the second Great Awakening failed to resolve the tension within the religious promise itself, and between the democratic, universalist thrust of revival religion and secular society. Woman's social sphere was expanded, but only as an extension of the moral authority of the home. Only radical secular ideologists such as Fanny Wright and Robert Dale Owens and theological radicals such as John Humphrey Noyes and the Shakers recognized that the conflict of ideals over the place of women in society could not be resolved by reform. Nothing short of complete institutional transformation would be successful.

Religion and the Family: The Tension between American Protestantism and Secular Social Change

The veneration of the family as an ideal had been maintained from the time of early American Puritanism through the nineteenth century and was supported by (1) a legal system that held the family as a corporate entity with the husband as its head and legal representative, and the wife as its heart; (2) a normative system that firmly delineated the sphere and status of men, women, and children; and (3) a pervasive ecclesiastical system that not only elucidated these norms, but threatened sanctions beyond those of civil authority. This is, of course, an analytical distinction. It is impossible to realistically separate religious and civil authority in the seventeenth, eighteenth, and nineteenth centuries, for even when specific denominations were disestablished, the authority of the presbytery, synod, and parish were clearly recognized.

Arthur W. Calhoun's analysis of religion and the family, often tinged with excessive moral judgments, blames the Reformation and the Renaissance for the decline of the family as a social unit.[20] The elevation of the individual encouraged every man to stand on his own two feet, and the laxity of opinion and teaching on divorce and the sacredness of marriage first set men free to violate social standards: "rights magnified; duties approached zero." Received revelation gave birth to sects such as the Anabaptists of Munster, who encouraged polygamy, and permitted the "looseness" of the Quakers, who entered into marriage without the intervention of clergy.

The Puritan believed that if the human race had only followed God's commandments from the beginning it would have never needed churches and civil governments as means of social control. In God's original plan, man was to live innocently and happily with no need for social organization beyond the family. With evil awakened in the world, there arose the need for stronger means of control. The authority of state and church, in Aristotelian fashion, was prefigured in the family. Adam's authority over his family was the embryo of state authority and the seed of the church was found in the Edenic adoration that Adam and Eve offered God.[21] The family provided more than just the template for the Puritan social order. It was the fundamental element of the commonwealth.

We have already noted the conflict between individualism and commonwealth.[22] The availability of cheap land and an expanding economy impaired the old-fashioned structure of the family and undermined religiously based communal values, often removing the youngest generation from the local family and community circle. Liberalization of divorce laws further weakened the religious community's hold on the family. Rejecting the sacramental theory of marriage and establishing marriage as a civil rite, New England Puritanism broadened the grounds for divorce beyond adultery and desertion to include numerous other marital offenses.[23]

Throughout the nineteenth century, American Protestants continued to revere the family, but other social forces acted to transform its structure and chip away at its authority. Tocqueville observed that democracy did much more than increase American individualism: "When the condition of society becomes democratic and men adopt as their general principle that it is good and lawful to judge all things for oneself, using former points of belief not as a rule of faith, but simply as a means of information, the power which the opinions of the father exercise over those of his sons diminishes as well as his legal power."[24] Democracy's effects were not completely destructive to the family. As legal aspects of parental authority declined with the demise of aristocracy, the relations between fathers and children became more intimate and affectionate.

Industrialization, individualism, and the decline of household manufacturing further altered the family in that its economic activity now took place beyond the walls and supervision of the household. This was particularly significant for women and children, because once they entered the mill or factory, the authority of the foreman, not the husband or father, applied. Certainly women gained no great level of freedom on entering the factory, for their wages were low and their household responsibilities were still considerable, but their sphere was extended and a small measure of independence was granted to those whose autonomy had been swallowed by marriage.[25]

Children were valued as the reservoir of hope for struggling parents—as farm and household hands and as income producers—but industrialization also emancipated youth by providing the opportunity for making one's way alone. In the cities, working mothers were seldom able to look closely after their children. Foreign visitors, native newspapers, and popular magazines decried the precocity of children, their destructiveness, irreverence, independence, the cocksureness of young boys, and the decline of parental authority.

Second Great Awakening preachers recognized the economic and political forces that seemed to be chipping away at the authority of the family and vigorously demanded the revitalization of the household as a moral force. The healthy and pious family, they argued, should not merely be a refuge from the competition and corruption of the world; it must be a moral core from which reform radiated into the world. The temperance and moral reform movements that grew out of revivalism, particularly those aimed at prostitution and licentiousness in general, were not merely attempts to restore the family; they utilized the family as a moralizing force in the world, as an instrument for bringing the world into line with religious principles, for transcending the tension between religion and world.

The second Great Awakening also had contrary effects that stemmed from the nature of religious enthusiasm. The family might have been the smallest unit of the Puritan commonwealth, but at the prayer and revival meetings individuals were saved one by one, regardless of the religious status of the rest of the family. At the height of a revival the family tension between the "saved" and the resistant or stubborn was surely formidable. Revivals could split the family along sectarian lines. The newly regenerate might revolt against the orthodoxies of the family's local parish or be converted by an alien sect.

This chapter has not been interested in totaling the pluses and minuses and coming out with a revivalist "bottom line" asserting the strengthening or weakening of the family. The concern has been to point out the conflicts within religion and between religion and world. In examining the relationship between religion and sex, women, and the family, we have uncovered three fundamental tensions that were not resolved by the second Great Awakening. First, we have elaborated American Protestantism's sexual ambivalence. From the Puritan commonwealth to the second Great Awakening there had been a clear understanding of sex as a human necessity—as enjoyable, healthy, natural, and God-given. But alongside these sentiments stood a religiously inspired repressiveness that viewed sex as a potential threat to piety and the social fabric. The sexual siren could lure the pious and civic minded away from their religious and social responsibilities and foster spiritual, familial, and communal decay. American Victorianism and revivalism tapped this repressive vein and elaborated the ideals of the "Christian gentleman" and the cult of "true womanhood."

Second, these Victorian-evangelical sex roles were laden with their own tensions. The discipline, self-control, and propriety of the "Christian gentleman" clashed with an older ethos of the aggressive, only partially controllable male sexuality. The cult of "true womanhood" was just as problematic. The practical demands of farm, factory, and home, and frontier and city put the realization of ideal femininity beyond the reach of all save the monied classes. Furthermore, the womanly ideal contained its own contradiction. If women were the protectors of morals, religion, and the family, why should their influence be restricted to the home? The benevolent movements of the second Great Awakening unleashed woman's "angelic nature" against secular corruption and vice, but only as an extension of the moral authority of the home. Woman's "separate sphere" had been stretched, but it remained intact.

Third, American Protestantism has always revered the family, but in the nineteenth century, democracy, industrialization, urbanization, and the advance of the frontier strengthened American individualism and eroded the authority of the family. Second Great Awakening preachers vigorously demanded the revitalization of the family, but revivalism often split families over sectarian lines or between regenerate and unregenerate kin because Scripture counseled turning from one's family to follow the faith. These three tensions provided the basis for John Humphrey Noyes's sexual and familial ideology, and their resolution was critical to his mission: to introduce the kingdom of heaven on earth.[26]

According to Noyes, worldly marriage was a fundamental obstacle to following two basic tenets of Christianity: the love of God and the universal love of man. Monogamous sexuality not only prevented one from loving one's neighbor, it also stood in the way of complete enjoyment of God's gift of sensual pleasure. Noyes fully rejected American Protestantism's sexual ambivalence. He accepted sex as normal, natural, pleasurable, and healthy, as did many of his contemporaries, but he went further: sex itself was a religious experience, a sacrament through which the partners loved God and each other, and absorbed spiritual energy in a single act. Rather than being a threat to religious devotion and piety, it was its fullest expression. Universal love as practiced in the kingdom of heaven, according to Noyes's interpretation of Paul, knew no structural limits and embraced all souls in a communism of spiritual and sexual love. Initiation of the kingdom of heaven on earth required the abolition of all artificial boundaries to human love. Worldly marriage, as it was then practiced, was a cultural form appropriate to an earlier religious era. In the heretofore unrecognized Christian age of fulfillment, monogamous marriage was an anachronistic restraint of humankind's amative potential. Complex marriage, a collective familial form in which all community members are "married to all others," was Noyes's social invention that would transcend the tension between religion and sex, the family and gender roles.

The family as it was then constituted would also require extensive changes to make it compatible with the universal love and communism of the kingdom of heaven on earth. For Noyes, the family promoted private property, capitalism, and a selfish economic life diametrically opposed to the communism of the primitive Church, the inspiration for his kingdom of heaven on earth. Without the strict cultural delineation of the family as the fundamental unit of economic life, the traditional and rational justifications for private property and exclusive accumulation of wealth could disintegrate. Furthermore, complex marriage would mitigate the tensions between the family and industrialization, and restore the "family" to a central role in the productive process. The community's productive and distributive facilities and labor force would be coterminous with the "extended family" under complex marriage.

Noyes clearly recognized that the plight of women was inextricably bound to the patriarchal monogamous family and the cultural, political, and economic institutions that provided its support. Within conventional marriage, women were reduced to the status of property, submissive to their husbands' will and relegated to a stifling domestic sphere regardless of their abilities or inclinations. The contradictions that stemmed from their hearth-based inferior status and their role as angelic defender of morals, religion, and family could only be eliminated by eliminating patriarchy in the collective family and granting full spiritual and social equality to women. Such equality included participation in all levels of community social, political, and economic life. Noyes believed that God and the individual personality were composed of both masculine and feminine traits. Social convention prevented men and women from developing the balance of "masculinity" and "femininity" by depreciating the characteristic of the opposite gender in one's own sex. The role contradiction that ensnared both men and women could be resolved by first granting full equality for women; by recognizing the importance of the "feminine nature" for male character and the "male nature" for female character; and by allowing each to achieve a natural equilibrium.

It is strikingly ironic that the religious source of the Oneida Community's theory of women's rights has the same Pauline roots as the Christian misogynous tradition. Christian misogyny, according to Noyes, had its source in scriptural interpretation that missed or ignored the important role of women in the primitive Church. Women were present at and important to all the miracles of the New Testament. Jesus' first miracle, the turning of water to wine, was done at the encouragement of his mother. It should also be remembered that Mary Magdalene was the first to know of the resurrection and served as an intermediary between Christ and the apostles by relating the news; she was thus the first to preach the Gospel.[27]

5
The Tension between Religion and Science

Science held a unique position in the thought of John Humphrey Noyes. Of all the social and cultural forms and pursuits of Americans, only science, as it was then conceived and practiced, would remain intact in the kingdom of heaven on earth. Contemporary political, economic, sexual, and familial life would all be transcended by higher forms more appropriate to the age of Christian fulfillment. Noyes, along with most of his religiously minded contemporaries, looked to science for rational support of revelation and inspiration and for more profound knowledge of God's work; but he parted company with the religious establishment in the 1860s when his study of Charles Darwin and Francis Galton (a pioneer of eugenics) suggested that the principles of evolution and genetics could be applied to the spiritual, intellectual, and physical improvement of humankind. Selective breeding, Noyes claimed, could be used to create the more spiritual and perfectible new men and women that would inhabit the kingdom of heaven on earth. Under Noyes's direction, the Oneida Community pledged its reproductive capacity to the pursuit of science and human improvement in a program called "stirpiculture."[1]

The first half of the nineteenth century—the years when the thought of John Humphrey Noyes crystallized and the Oneida Community was organized—was a period of little tension between religion and science. Although the rational demands of science have always driven its practitioners toward a characteristic worldview and theories independent of or at odds with religious beliefs, it was not until the organizational, theoretical, and technological developments of the 1860s that the principled opposition to religious presuppositions became something more than a minority voice in America. An autonomous science then became a powerful competitor to a theologically restrained science. The Oneida Community's commitment to science and its practice of sending talented young members to universities to study meant that this new approach, that of no longer viewing science as handmaiden to religion, would filter into the community. Chapter 8 examines how science came to undermine religious belief and became a focal point for conflict within the Oneida Community.

Max Weber's ideas on the relationship between science and religion will provide the theoretical underpinnings for our analysis. We will account for the absence of tension between religion and science prior to the 1860s, and then examine the changes in both organized religion and science that help explain the emergence of tension between these spheres.

Max Weber and the Tension between Religion and Science

Frequently, and particularly in the case of ascetic Protestantism, religion considers purely empirical research, including natural science, a more favorable bedfellow than philosophy, which has often pulled out the bedding in skepticism. And, as we shall see later, science has often reinforced religion, furnishing a sacred worldview with empirical props. Through the empirical sciences one could attain a far deeper understanding of God's work and Scripture. In short, a religiously informed—and constrained—science increases and serves God's glory by fulfilling his commandments. This was particularly true for Calvinism and similarly inspired sects committed to inner-worldly asceticism. Calvinism demanded that one lead an alert and intelligent life, bringing order to existence by destroying impulsive enjoyment and idleness and fulfilling God's will through diligence in a "calling." These ethical and behavioral prescriptions meshed well with emerging modern science. Physics came to be the favorite science of Puritanism in that it permitted one to inquire beyond that which was revealed in Scripture, to know God's works more deeply, yet still steer clear of skepticism, irreverence, and heresy.

Max Weber observed that science would also stand in thorough-going tension with religion, especially when science took its most rational form.[2] A self-conscious tension between religion and intellectual knowledge has arisen "wherever rational, empirical knowledge has consistently worked through to the disenchantment of the world and its transformation into a causal mechanism." Religion, and especially salvation religion, offers the postulate that the world is somehow God-ordained, the cosmos being meaningfully and ethically oriented. Empirically and mathematically oriented science counters with the negation of all intellectual approaches that seek a nonmaterial, unverifiable "meaning" for inner-worldly occurrences. As we witness an increase in rationalism in empirical science, we see that religion is pushed further and further into the realm of the irrational, until it ultimately becomes the manifestation and archetype of the irrational itself. Here Weber established the tension between religion and science on both epistemological and valuative grounds. Science and religion are literally "worlds apart" in terms of the directions of their rationality and their goals. Not only does the logic of the pursuit of valid scientific knowledge clash with religion; science and religion also represent mutually exclusive value orientations and worldviews.

For Weber the stark ideal-typical contrasts between science and religion did not rule out the contextual elements that vary and determine the consistency and self-consciousness of this tension. These factors shaping the relationship between religion and intellectual life are almost exhaustively explored in Weber's comparative historical analyses of the world religions and civilizations, but he finds it is impossible to totally eliminate the tension between religion and world, for it ultimately rests upon different images of the world. Religion claims to unlock the meaning of the world by charisma and illumination rather than by intellect and empirical analysis. The question of "ultimacy" is not as one-sidedly idealistic as it seems. We must remember that "world images" are not merely the result of ideas; they also reflect the political, cultural, and structural milieu of their bearers. For example, the worldly images of a priesthood are not simply determined by the content and organization of their religious ideas; they also include their structural, cultural, and economic status vis-à-vis other groups, i.e., whether they are socially "privileged," politically influential, and so forth. The same holds for intellectuals in general, as Weber suggests in the example of his contemporary German intelligentsia adopting religious, mystical, or romantic views of the world as a consequence of their political impotence and frustration.[3]

These theoretical points raise the substantive questions of when and under what conditions does the tension between religion and the intellectual sphere—in our case, science—become consistent and self-conscious; how has science come to successfully claim to represent the only possible reasoned view of the world; and how and under what circumstances has religion receded in the face of the competing claims of science?

The Harmony between Science and Protestantism in America

Eighteenth-century America was awash with enthusiasm. It was ionized by the religious excitement of the Great Awakening and the contrary current of Enlightenment rationalism that served to pull mind and spirit in different directions. In spite of the secular thrust of the Enlightenment, religion was not filtered out of intellectual life. Secular confidence about life in the world and the progress of mankind often raised doubt or caused revision of ideas about life in the hereafter. Benjamin Franklin, a Deist, believed in a "first mover and maker" of the universe who set the planets and stars in motion according to universal laws. The Deity was not only the most perfect being, he was also a divine mathematician.[4]

The ethics of Puritanism and science were both compatible and mutually reinforcing.[5] Rationalism was put forward as a restraint on the passions, and Puritanism lent a sympathetic attitude to those "callings" that demanded a constant application of rigorous reasoning. Conversely, science's utility, its empiricism, and its requirements of continuous, regimented, disciplined activity were congenial to Puritan tastes. Although the Puritan ethic was consonant with certain basic attributes of science, it also provided its severest restraint. Science was not extolled as an end in itself but as an effective means of promoting the glory of God, the alpha and omega of man's worldly activity.

The Puritans and Deists were not alone in their respect for science. Brooke Hindle and, more recently, E. Digby Baltzell have pointed out that the affinity of Puritanism with science that Robert Merton found in seventeenth-century England could be similarly, if not more strongly, seen in American Quakerism in spite of Quaker antipathy for higher education. The internal nature of the Quaker ethic included a positive attitude toward the study of nature, a rational and empirical approach to thought, and prohibitions against "fashionable amusements and diversions." Religious authority, tradition, and even the Bible could not be held above direct experience in the Quaker creed.[6]

Natural philosophy required a thorough training in mathematics and was, therefore, entirely out of reach of most laypeople and Quakers. Thus the Boston Puritan took the lead in this area. To the Puritan mind learning and godliness were inseparable and Harvard College was the symbol of that fusion. Natural history was more conducive to the Quaker mind. Diligence, discipline, hard work, and close attention to detail, allied with a thorough knowledge of the Linnaean system of botanical classification, were all that was needed to distinguish oneself in American botany at the time. To most Quakers, theory was as useless as theology. Systematic collection of facts accommodated their preference for things over words.

An even stronger link can be established between science and "Old School" Presbyterianism. Antebellum America possessed a growing interest in both science *and* evangelical Protestantism, and embraced the idea that science and religion, Baconianism and the Bible, were engaged in similar enterprises directed toward the same ends.[7] Baconian Presbyterianism portrayed scientific investigation as an aid to piety, the method of induction useful in establishing the truth of the creation and the authenticity of the Christian promise. Biblical accounts could be analyzed as evidence and processed inductively. The witnesses to biblical events certainly were not scientific observers, but the inductive method could be used to uncover their essential truth. The idea that science was to be the handmaiden of religion was not limited to the Old School Presbyterians. By the nineteenth century this position was common to all Protestant sects save those that rejected secular knowledge outright.

In the eighteenth and nineteenh centuries, science's chief logical rival was theology. Both science and theology considered themselves to be delving into natural law. It is surprising that—despite the differences between evidence and revelation, induction and hermeneutics—there was little conflict between scientists and theologians. This can possibly be explained by a peculiarity of the relationship between the two professional groups: although theologians were the logical rivals of scientists, they were also the bearers of important cultural values to which scientists had to appeal and within which justify their professional and intellectual position. From America's founding until the twentieth century, theology and the oral culture of the pulpit held an overwhelming, if not hegemonic, influence over intellectual life. Scientific as well as political and economic thought depended upon theological support for its cultural legitimacy. This meant that any appearance of conflict had to be avoided. Naturally, the burden of avoiding conflict fell on the new profession. Science had to be defined and elaborated within the realm of the religious worldview; it had to refine, expand, and support theology without threatening to replace it. Every instance of order, of regularity, of lawfulness must lead to reinforced belief in the benevolence of God, the verity of Scripture, and the necessity of following God's law. The association of science with religion not only rendered legitimacy to science, it also gave society at large a stake in its pursuit. Science could be called upon to provide a nonspeculative, nonsectarian grounding for the authority of revelation.[8]

As science had yet to establish clear institutional and intellectual autonomy, the social circle to which scientists addressed themselves was not yet confined to an audience of like-minded colleagues sharing the same attitudes toward the means and ends of science.[9] Consequently, the narrower norms and values used to evaluate scientific scholarship were inflated to include the valuative foundations and logical "recipes" of the dominant intellectual ethos, i.e., Protestant theology. Scientific explanations and the scientific agenda itself were not solely determined by problems developing within science's logic and practice, but were dependent on theological considerations that permeated intellectual life. Of course there were other external considerations determining the scientific agenda, such as economic and technical needs, but these did not restrict scientists in terms of the nature of scientific explanations or the kinds of scientific questions that could be addressed.

The restraints on science and the needs for consonance with religious ideas were not inflicted *upon* scientists, but *by* scientists on their own profession. The problem of the possible and probable tensions between science and religion was expressed in a continuous preoccupation with the harmony between science and religion. For example, Edward Hitchcock, a respected member of both professions, thus described the ideal man of science:

He is a man who loves Nature, and with untiring industry endeavors to penetrate her mysteries. With a mind too large for narrow views, too generous and frank for distorting prejudice, and too pure to be the slave of appetite and passion, he calmly surveys the phenomena of nature, to learn from thence the great plan of the universe as it originally lay in the Divine mind.

Nor does he stop when he has found out the mechanical, chemical, and organic laws of nature, but rises to those higher principles by which the moral relations of man to his Maker are disclosed. Hence he receives with gratitude and joy those richer disclosures of truth which revelation brings. To its authority he bows reverently and rejoicingly, and counts it the best use he can make of science to render it tributary to revelation and to the cultivation of his own piety. He exhibits a generous enthusiasm in the cultivation of science; but he has a stronger desire to have it associated with religion . . . and we may be sure that whatever goes by the name of science, which contradicts a fair and enlightened exhibition of revealed truth, is only false philosophy.[10]

In a similar vein, James Dwight Dana, a New York–born geologist, zoologist, and the son of a Congregationalist minister, assures us that science had never claimed to explain the ultimate nature of life, nor was it presumptuous enough to think it could. Those who thought otherwise held a "fatal misconception of science."[11] Those who claimed science opened access to higher truths or could better explain life or creation were attacked foremost by scientists for violating their methodological canons and promoting ill will and hostility toward the profession.

Religion and the Theoretical and Normative Structure of Scientific Thought

Newton and, later, Bacon were the wellsprings of American science. Colonial science was characterized by a passion for Newtonian science to the exclusion of continental advances. It was not until after the War of 1812 that the intellectual spell of England was broken. In New England the infatuation with Newton was manifest in the practical involvements of shippers and merchants with astronomy, navigation, and geography. "The path to these sciences went through Newton's *Principia*."[12] His mechanics was the first example of modern science in its finest development; as a convincing set of axioms, a logical method, a developed technique, and an ability to forecast events.

As one would expect, the success of Newton's theory of gravity in predicting the movements of heavenly bodies had a theological impact and also provided more precise navigational and geographical measurement. Celestial symmetry and universal laws suggested an independent and rational confirmation of religious beliefs. While many argued that astronomy was useless and had no pragmatic benefits, others considered it to be the "perfect science." The other sciences would have to modify or wholly change the expression of their laws, but once the fundamental principles of the planets and stars were discovered, one could sit back and admire the perfect contemplative science. The natural laws of science enabled Americans to look upon God "without superstitious terror," and approach him "without fanatical familiarity or mystical enthusiasm."[13] By the time of independence from Britain, the dominant conception of science held by the educated was that of a passive contemplation of divine perfection revealed in the eternal order and coherence of nature.

Baconian inductive philosophy thrived in the antimetaphysical atmosphere of early nineteenth-century America. Induction was held to be nearly synonymous with classification. Once a piece of data was clearly located in the "natural system" it would yield its complete store of scientific knowledge. Not only did this agree with America's pragmatic sentiments oriented toward sensed fact, it also supported its pervasive interest in natural history and mineralogy. These areas were particularly fertile for American science because no specialized technical education or mathematics was required, and the tremendous number of heretofore unknown indigenous flora provided the opportunity for challenging, ground-breaking work and the building of international reputations.

Once science began to turn its attention to that which was not immediately evident or accessible to observation in its most unsophisticated form, once such phenomena began to be considered "data," Baconian science was hamstrung. Questions of how elements combined, the phlogiston theory and the discovery of oxygen, and questions of what was light, heat, matter, electricity, and magnetism could not be addressed within the Baconian paradigm. Scientists began to pay lip service to Baconianism in routine ritualized introductory tributes, but proceeded to spin "speculative" theories divorced from it.[14]

Certainly the decline of crude Baconian empiricism did not purge religion from science, but consideration of such "imponderables" as light, heat, electricity, and magnetism introduced a modern conception of theory, hypothesis, and informed scientific speculation.[15] Once these became entrenched in historical geology, and analysis came to replace classification as the way of science, the submerged conflict between religion and science came to the surface.

The "imponderables" required other means of understanding the world; simple demonstration and induction proved inadequate. A method of leaping from the known to the unknown had to be found and "analogy" was called upon to allow inferences to be made that went significantly beyond the "facts." Just as Baconian empiricism and induction were ideologically bound to religion, this new scientific tool, "analogy," was also forged in a furnace stoked by religion. The unity of God's plan allows one to reason from what is observed to what is not observed, or to what cannot be observed with confidence, because the architecture of God's creation is consistently based on an all-encompassing blueprint. It is significant that these ideas were not foisted upon science by the clergy or religious zealots, but arose within the scientific community that was bent on demonstrating the verity of a God-ordained world and its own piety.[16]

What we have exposed here is the metatheoretical structure of nineteenth-century science: the underlying assumptions as to the nature and purpose of science, what can be recognized as "data," what is the logical process by which data are evaluated, what is "fact" and "observation," and what inferences can be drawn from them. We have seen that as observation, data, and facticity changed to accommodate the imponderables, the underlying normative structure remained the same. Science could only make sense within a God-ordained, ordered, symmetrical, and harmonious universe. Science could only be conceived as a means of comprehending the divine order of the universe utilizing the God-given gift of reason. For much of the first half of the nineteenth century American science possessed little intellectual autonomy from religion and was generally perceived as a servant to religion, providing rational support for Protestantism. We must also remember that the beginning of the nineteenth century was also a period of tremendous religious enthusiasm.

Among other traits, both the first and second Great Awakenings were characterized by an intense commitment to religious emotionalism stirred up by itinerant New Light preachers in large, often protracted, revivals that embraced whole towns. Revivalists such as Charles Grandison Finney attempted conversion of the masses using fire and brimstone diatribes against the sinfulness of man in general and the spiritual bankruptcy of a clergy more inclined toward an intellectual theology than the base of "true" religion—emotion and purity of heart. Romantic and intensely dramatic presentation challenged the academic rhetoric and logic of the established clergy. The revivalists insisted that formal theology leads only to divisiveness, and speculative systems only to dissension. The evangelical method must address itself to the heart. The revivalists were first and foremost oriented toward concrete results, which they measured by the level of emotional enthusiasm raised and the number of conversions claimed. Evangelical distrust of intellectualism reinforced American pragmaticism and bridled pure theology—theory with no immediate practical application.

Richard H. Shyrock has claimed that the accepted explanations of the apparent American indifference to scientific theory in the nineteenth century are severely lacking.[17] The unavailability of European theoretical science; the American preoccupation with subduing the frontier and conquering a continent; Tocqueville's combination of democracy and economic opportunity; and clerical control of the colleges and universities are all significant, but all fall short of accounting for the neglect of basic theoretical science. This pragmatism seemed to emerge with the growing complexity, technical sophistication, specialization, and professionalization of science. In eighteenth-century America, science was relatively nontechnical and cultivated by self-taught men pursuing it in their spare time. If their interests were abstract or impractical, it was solely their own concern. Thus early American scientists such as David Rittenhouse, Benjamin Rush, and Benjamin Franklin could work at science motivated by an idle curiosity. But between 1800 and 1850, when science became more technical, specialized, and professional, when people came to pursue science as a means of livelihood, idle curiosity gave way to practical technological results.

The decline of the relatively aristocratic aspects of American society and the development of relatively democratic features between 1780 and 1830 saw the decline of the wealthy gentleman devoted to pure scientific research. The ascension of the business class infused science with a utilitarian spirit. The mercantile nouveaux riches neglected or were unable to cultivate the genteel tradition of the colonial elite as the growing complexity and tempo of commerce absorbed more and more of their time and interest. The most ruthless and materialist tycoon could enjoy the arts, but would stop short of supporting the idle curiosity of scientists when their results became more and more inaccessible to the scientifically unsophisticated. As time became money, interest in immediate results grew and basic research waned.

All that Shyrock says is familiar to those acquainted with America's rise as a business civilization, but he has isolated science and business from the other enthusiasm of the period, i.e., religion. We must not forget that science was just beginning to emerge as an autonomous institution in this period. As American intellectual life was dominated by the pulpit (if not directly, then through its descendants and dissidents) it would be rather surprising if a nascent science, yet to establish its own cultural legitimacy, would strike out in a direction directly opposed to the currents of religious enthusiasm. In this period, science merely reflected a powerful religiously based antipathy toward intellectualism in general and theoretical speculation in particular. As Richard Hofstadter has noted in the recent past (and Finney in his own time), anti-intellectual sentiments were not directed at the clergy alone, but were also intended as a broad religiously inspired cultural critique of America by the New Lighters.[18]

Even those scientists who eschewed economic and pragmatic motivations voiced them nonetheless to convince the skeptics. The United States Exploring Expedition, more commonly known as the Wilkes Expedition, which departed for the Antarctic on August 18, 1838, included some of America's finest professional scientific minds, but the project could not be justified on the basis of science alone. In Jeremiah Reynolds's (the corresponding secretary of the expedition) letter to President Jackson on November 16, 1836, he duly notes the scientific importance of the mission and then stresses the "primary importance" of its economic benefits chiefly in terms of vegetable production, the transplanting of vegetable products from the countries explored, and other "important accessions to our sources of national wealth and com[fort]," which would, no doubt, include the fur trade.[19]

This then is the normative structure and religious milieu within which science and scientists operated in the first half of the nineteenth century. A situation existed in which science had little institutional autonomy or cultural acceptance in its own right and depended upon support from the religious sector for cultural approval in return for legitimizing a sacred universe. This was also the normative structure of science that prevailed among John Humphrey Noyes and the first generation of Oneida communists. Because the spheres of science and religion were not autonomous institutions and worldviews, and because the scientific worldview had yet to exclude religious beliefs as a matter of epistemological principle, Noyes and his early followers could warmly embrace science as the servant of religion, and as a means to individual and collective perfection. The second-generation communists, we shall see, were educated in a different intellectual milieu. They had been raised as Perfectionists, but at Yale they came in contact with a science that tried to solve nature's puzzles without recourse to the divine, and often challenged religious belief with a persuasive independent logic and methodology. It is time to examine the broadening cultural acceptance of science in the nineteenth century and its increasing institutional development. In this fashion we will expose the factors that brought science and religion into an acute state of tension in the second half of the century, and set the background to the generational rift we will discover at the Oneida Community.

The Maturation of American Science

The opening of the Revolutionary War initiated a tremendous burst of scientific activity in America, particularly in engineering and inventions to supply the troops, and in medicine to patch them together. The increase in sea trade and shipbuilding that followed the end of the Navigation Acts' restraints required ever-finer navigational tools and techniques based upon advanced mathematics and astronomy. The New England coast provided a fertile niche for self-taught mathematicians, astronomers, cartographers, and clock-makers, and New England's science remained for a long time the science of a mercantile class bent on techniques and inventions to speed its ships and cargo.

The navigational science of the time was Newtonian, and the post-revolutionary mercantile interests that leaned toward England and Federalism provided an ideological barrier to the French contribution. Natural science, geology, zoology, and mineralogy held little practical interest for merchants or skippers and their indifference was heightened to antipathy by its French, democratic flavor. The clergy was still powerful in the colleges and was often equally antipathetic. Anything French was associated with excessive democratic zeal, free-thinking, and atheism. When the political winds of the French Revolution brought Albert Gallatin, Joseph Priestly, Thomas Cooper, Pierre Adet, and Du Pont de Nemours to America, their arrival was agreeable to the Jeffersonians and anathema to the Federalists. It took John Adams himself to restrain his secretary of state from prosecuting Joseph Priestly under the Alien and Sedition Acts.

Where partisan sentiments pushed science in a particular direction, the rising tide of nationalism after the Revolution advanced its cultural acceptance. The early decades of the nineteenth century were an extremely fertile period for western science. Pierre Laplace, James Joule, André Ampère, Justus von Liebig, Hermann von Helmholtz, Alexander Herschel, Antoine Lavoisier, Edmund Davy,

Frederick Hutton, and Jean Lamarck were in the vanguard of European science, but American science had few outstanding figures. American naturalists made great contributions to their field and were widely acclaimed by their European colleagues, but the new republic lagged far behind in most other areas. The more apparent it was that America had few, if any, scientific minds that could compare with the Europeans, the greater the embarrassment became. Not only did America long for a science "equal in majesty to the colossal expanse of its landscape," its failings led to a compensatory scorn of the more contemplative, theoretical, and abstract scientific pursuits.[20]

By the end of the War of 1812, it seemed to many that America was on its way to solving some of the most basic problems standing in the way of its intellectual development. Real political independence had been achieved, nation building appeared to be an unqualified success, cities were growing, and a slow and uncertain communication and transportation network was improving. American speechmakers were brimming with optimism over the material and scientific potentials to be realized. Patriotic and utilitarian appeals were not sufficient to drum up popular support for the sciences. Its spokesmen stressed the moral and religious benefits of this, the highest form of rational amusement. Even with growing acceptance, propelled by independence and nationalism, science was still not ready to ground claims to cultural validity solely on its own merits; the organization and professional structure of science was still relatively weak.

By the early nineteenth century, the era of scientific leadership by dilettantes had come to an end. Broadening cultural acceptance linked with its firm entrenchment in academe led to a significant growth in the complexity of scientific knowledge. Increased theoretical, mathematical, and technical sophistication estranged the talented amateur and well-educated layperson from scientists and the intricate details of their work. While the alienation from the substance of science did not check the overall enthusiasm, the public was reduced to a facile enjoyment of the "wonders" and "marvels" of their universe.

In natural history, the Linnaean system of classification based upon obvious, easily identifiable physical characteristics gave way to the natural system requiring comparison of a large number of relations to arrive at an "overall affinity"; a judgment possible only to a trained expert. Similarly, as chemistry, geology, and mineralogy advanced, classification gave way to analysis requiring specialized technical knowledge, and physics and astronomy increasingly made use of complex mathematical tools and sophisticated equipment.

The organizational development of American science did not begin in earnest until the decade before the Revolution. The American Philosophical Society, founded in 1769, drew together the intercolonial and intercontinental scientific interest. It was the American scientific community's most ambitious expression of cultural nationalism. Previous organizations were of a local nature. The founding and early leadership of the American Philosophical Society was in the hands of "peripheral Quakers, former Quakers, and near Quakers." Although constituting only a small minority of the Philadelphia population (about 13 percent), the Quakers succeeded beyond any other group in accumulating wealth, in leadership, the arts, and scientific work. In 1780, almost 120 years after King Charles II incorporated the Royal Society, the American Academy of Arts and Sciences was founded and it pledged itself "to cultivate every art and science which may tend to advance the interest, honor, dignity, and happiness of a free, independent, and virtuous people."[21]

Boston and Philadelphia had been the hubs of colonial science, Boston more provincial and Philadelphia more cosmopolitan, but public interest and scientific activity—including research, founding of societies and journals, and college and university chairs—began to spread throughout the nation.

In Europe, scientific research, coastal and geographical surveys, and other similar ventures were undertaken by princes. Such patronage was nonexistent in the United States, and the work of undemocratic agencies was distrusted. The lack of federal encouragement did not hold back or deflate the energies of American scientific pioneers. Benjamin Silliman, Frank Bigelow, Edward and James Dana, and others proceeded on as large a scale as possible in scientific organization and surveys.

From 1830 on, the states, becoming conscious of the nation's treasures, took the initiative. Massachusetts, Tennessee, Maryland, New Jersey, Connecticut, Virginia, Maine, New York, Ohio, Pennsylvania, Delaware, Indiana, Michigan, New Hampshire, Rhode Island, Alabama, South Carolina, and Vermont were all surveyed and a vast amount of geological, mineralogical, botanical, and zoological material was collected between 1830 and 1844. The federal government followed the lead of the states reluctantly. In 1832, Jefferson's long-dormant Coast Survey was reorganized, and this began the great era of coastal surveys that peaked in the 1840s. By the middle of the 1840s, public and private funds were available to a growing body of scientists who drew support from a newly devoted public anxious for the material and spiritual benefits of modern science.

Enthusiastic enlightened opinion widened public acceptance of science and elevated the status of scientists. The nineteenth-century American public took kindly to lectures on chemistry and geology, despite the occasional frowns of the clergy. Popular lectures became an integral part of the "public" aspects of scientific life. While the most profound scientific advances remained within the laboratory, professional journals, and private correspondence, the wonders and marvels of natural phenomena were offered for their educational, entertainment, and public-relations value at mechanics' institutes and scientific lyceums. Industrialists, farmers, mechanics, factory workers, and women all found something to spark their interest in the lectures and demonstrations of scientists and inventors: science had become democratized. Publicly sponsored science claimed it could promote the interests of all social strata.

The most significant impulse to theoretical science and its formal organization came from the estate of James Smithson, a wealthy English scientist. In the 1830s, when Congress was least ready to act, he bequeathed a half million dollars to the United States government to assist "the increase and diffusion of knowledge among men." The details of the organization were finally settled in 1844 and the Smithsonian Institution was created under the directorship of Joseph Henry. The institution emphasized the increase of knowledge rather than its diffusion, and work in ethnology, tropical biology, and astrophysics proliferated.

It can be seen that the first half of the nineteenth century was a period of tremendous scientific activity in the United States. Political and economic independence and an accompanying nationalism demanded that the new republic develop an intellectual reputation second to none. Philadelphia and Boston gave birth to early scientific organizations whose character increasingly became national, international, and professional. The leadership was taken over from the "natural philosophers" and amateurs by "scientists," and reflected their professional concerns and ambitions. Journals sprouted from these organizations and the number of periodicals publishing scientific material more than doubled between 1815 and 1825, from eleven to twenty-five. New York, Pennsylvania, and, to a lesser extent, Massachusetts and Ohio became centers of scientific publishing.

As nonprofessionals became less and less a part of the forefront of scientific activity, their interest and enthusiasm were catered to on the less-technical level. The practice and direction of science more and more gravitated to the specialized professionals, and science came to be viewed as a legitimate pursuit more for its utilitarian and material profit and less for its spiritual benefits, although the latter persisted as a firm ideological foundation.

The Emerging Tension between Religion and Science

Institutionalization contracted the scientific social circle and provided an organizational base, network, and outlet for scientists pursuing specialized problems. The scientist's critical audience, on which career and reputation depended, became composed of like-minded intellectuals and was oriented toward scientifically generated problems and explanations. With the increasing exclusion of amateurs and clerics from the core of scientific activity and organization, science began to generate theories that were independent of religious justifications and that were often in conflict with them. This was especially the case with geology and, later in the nineteenth century, evolutionary theory in biology. The day of theologically oriented scientists like Joseph Priestly was coming to a close.

The nineteenth century proved to be a productive period for American geology, but serious problems and controversies, both scientific and theological, lay ominously on the horizon. In late eighteenth- and early nineteenth-century England, competing explanations of the earth's origins clashed. "Catastrophists"—who saw Genesis as accurately recording the perfect description of nature and who believed that the surface and structure of the earth were determined by unique events issuing from God—were confronted by the growing ranks of "uniformitarians" who denied the literal accuracy of the Bible and explained the present condition of the earth as a result of continuous and uniform forces at work over a long period of time. By the 1830s this debate had emigrated to the United States and attracted scientific and theological partisans.

Benjamin Silliman (the first professional geologist in New England), Edward Hitchcock (a minister, Silliman's student, and the former president of Amherst College), and James Dwight Dana of Yale all grappled with the dialectic of geology and Scripture, suggest-

ing that perhaps the Bible should be accepted as a code of moral instruction rather than a scientific text. Their leanings toward scientific
criteria of evidence did not, however, prevent them from engaging in
strained hermeneutic acrobatics that kept them from rejecting the
biblical account outright.[22] It is no surprise that the rationalizations
and theological tap dances of scientists resolved nothing. They were
applauded by liberals, attacked by conservatives. After 1859, the
combat shifted to the Darwinian controversy and escalated. Once
again an American scientist sought to reconcile the two sides.

Jean Louis Rodolphe Agassiz—a Swiss natural historian who emigrated to the United States in 1846 and was considered a "giant" of
American science—was a staunch opponent of evolutionary theory
and natural selection. Asa Gray—the most renowned American bot-
anist of the period and a close colleague of Agassiz—attempted to
reason away the differences between the "creationist" and "evolu-
tionist" in his review of Darwin's *Origin of Species*.

Agassiz was convinced that each species originated simultaneously and generally in the geographical region it currently occupied in
perhaps the same numbers as there was at any subsequent period.
Darwin maintained a common descent of individuals of a species,
not only from a single birthplace, but from a single ancestor or pair.
Species would establish themselves through natural agencies. In the
apparent stark contrast between the two theories, Gray found only
differences in degree, not kind: "The ordinary view—rendering unto
Caesar the things that are Caesar's—looks to natural agencies for
the actual distribution and perpetuation of species, to a supernatural
one for their origin. . . . The theory of Agassiz regards the origin of
species and their present distribution over the world as equally pri-
mordial, equally supernatural; that of Darwin as equally derivative,
equally natural."[23]

Gray called Agassiz to task for being "theistic to excess," because
attributing the origin and distribution of species to divine will moves
us out of the domain of inductive science. He also found Darwin
equally problematic. Although his method is strictly scientific, his
theory can only be proved indirectly. Where Agassiz views the phenomena in question only in relation to the divine mind, Darwin seeks
to take natural causes as far as he can. Gray was an early advocate of
Darwinianism in America but he was also an apologist for the harmony of science and revealed religion, and he was torn between two
colleagues; neither could be abandoned without exacerbating the
split within the scientific community or stirring up outside hostility

from liberal or conservative elements. The path of least resistance beckoned and Gray diplomatically stressed the common points of both theories and tried to defuse the apparent conflict by locating their approaches on two distinct levels. Agassiz was considering only the ultimate *why*, Darwin the proximate *why* or *how*. In a final feat of theoretical fence-sitting in an appeal to scientific progress, Gray claimed that the theories of neither Agassiz nor Darwin necessarily excluded the other. It was the task and hope of future investigation to see them merged.[24]

The strained ratiocinations of Gray and his ad hoc defusing of the conflict suggest that the previous recipes for maintaining harmony between science and religion were no longer digestible, and the traditional time-worn appeals to serving the glory of God by illuminating his works through reason no longer satisfied. The distended rationalizations of Benjamin Silliman, James Dwight Dana, and Asa Gray became increasingly transparent—if not implausible—as science refined its logic and methodology and gradually pushed religion beyond its area of concern. That such distinguished scientists persisted in reaching for theological toeholds to support their science indicates how firmly entrenched its religious foundation was, and how hopeless the prospects of mediation seemed to be. Gray's efforts, at the beginning of the Darwinian controversy, express hope but suggest despair and resignation in that the logic wedding science and religion had clearly become bankrupt.

Revivalism, Anti-Intellectualism, and Clerical Decline

As scientists had been gaining in institutional organization, prestige, and authority, their intellectual competitors, the clergy, had begun a slow, gradual decline in the early seventeenth century. Insofar as a Puritan theocracy ever existed in America, it failed almost at once. Economic individualism, political localism, religious provincialism, and sectarian diversity stunted the development of any unified religious system and dispersed ministerial authority. The settlement of a wide variety of immigrant groups with their own brand of Christian confession made certain that a monopolistic religious establishment could never exist. New England Protestantism was divided along sectarian lines of Congregationalism, Presbyterianism, Anabaptism, antinomianism, and the independents; and along doctrinal lines over predestination, infant baptism, the Half-Way Covenant, and "preparation" for salvation by the middle of the seventeenth century.

Pushing the American public to unprecedented levels of religious excitement and enthusiasm, the Great Awakenings of the eighteenth and nineteenth centuries weakened the hold of traditional doctrines, exacerbated sectarian diversity, and struck severe blows at clerical intellectualism and authority. Religious emotionalism and the experience of salvation eclipsed Puritan rationalism and formalism as the alpha and omega of religiosity. Old School preachers were denounced by the New Lighters as cold and religiously empty, having given up the "true" religion of the heart for an ersatz conviction based on dogma and intellectualism.

Sidney Mead explores the institutional decline of the Puritan clergy in terms of the growing evangelical conception of the ministry.[25] Beginning with the fading of sacerdotal aspects of the ministry through the Great Awakenings, evangelicism moved from a minority voice in American Protestantism to dominance around 1850. The universalism of the evangelical wave devalued sacrament, dogma, and clerical intellectualism in favor of the emotionalism of "spirit." With this new emphasis we find not only a strong anti-intellectual movement among clergy but a diffusion of ministerial roles. Parish ministers, missionaries, secretaries of societies, teachers, and professors, and in some cases evangelists and revivalists all came to be viewed as legitimate ministerial positions. The diversification of the ministerial calling further devalued clerical intellectualism; such concerns were widely seen as vestiges of a bygone age, out of step with the spirit of American Christianity. The clerical intelligentsia spoke less and less for the ministry in terms of theology and secular knowledge. During the very period when professionals were consolidating their monopoly over scientific knowledge, the clerical intellectual was receding in influence, and this recession crippled any effort to confront the threat of secular science.

The relative absence of conflict between science and religion in America prior to the 1850s was due to the cultural and intellectual hegemony of Protestantism and its clergy and to American science's technical, theoretical, professional, and institutional infancy.

Given the consonance between religion and science at the time, it is no surprise that John Humphrey Noyes and the Oneida Community could firmly embrace science as a manifestation of the continuing spiritual progress of mankind. It was only in the second half of the century, when science challenged religion and positivism looked for answers without homage to the divine, that the sacred and secular explanations parted ways. The conflict between perfection and science became one of the fundamental points of failure for John Humphrey Noyes's religious system. Young university-educated community members returned to Oneida with more than the specialized technical and scientific skills needed by community industries. Along with their knowledge of the physical sciences they brought an elaborate rational worldview incommensurable with the fundamental underpinnings of religious belief. Not all the young returned skeptics. Some were able to accommodate both worldviews without contradiction, but several, who the older generation had hoped would lead the community in the future, either openly espoused their doubts or atheism and withdrew, or lived within the community as quiet—and occasionally not so quiet—skeptics.

Part III
The Oneida Community:
A Utopian Resolution
of the Tension between
Religion and World

6
The Theology of John Humphrey Noyes

Ernest Lee Tuveson has found three kinds of utopian optimism underlying American ideology.[1] America has been perceived (1) as a retreat from the corruption of the old world; (2) as the place where the problems of history would be solved and its fruits disseminated, a benevolent empire; and (3) as the locale for the emergence of a new people possessed of a fresh and vital spirit. These convictions motivated the Massachusetts Bay Puritans, and, to nineteenth-century revivalists, they seemed on the verge of full realization.

Developing the ideas of John Wesley, Charles Grandison Finney —more than any other second Great Awakening preacher—established Perfectionism at the center of religious controversy. "Spiritual perfection," "sanctification," "holiness," or "entire consecration," as it was variously called, was not a blissful state reserved for the afterlife, but was thoroughly attainable in this world. The roads to the true Christian life and spiritual perfection were identical, for only the perfectly holy could hope to understand God's will and live up to his demands. Sanctification provided the "strength, stability, firmness, and perpetuity" of man's preference for the glory of God over his own self-interest. "The perfect control over all the moral movements of the mind brings a man back to where Adam was previous to the fall and constitutes perfect holiness." Sanctification was not the exclusive domain of religious virtuosos. It was the goal of all Christians. Those who are truly converted by a second baptism of the Holy Ghost "habitually live without sin and fall into sin only at intervals so few and far between that, in strong language, it may be said in truth they do not sin."[2]

Lyman Beecher was, as we have already noted, a staunch opponent of Finney's "Oberlin Perfectionism," particularly after it became associated with John Humphrey Noyes's "free-love" Perfectionism. In fact, Finney and Noyes differed on fundamental points. Self-control and the restraint of evil were the benchmarks of Finneyite perfection, and the revivalist felt that Noyes had dispensed with morality altogether.

Finney occupied center stage in the enthusiasm of the second Great Awakening, but other Perfectionist sects were influenced by, or benefited from, the theology and optimistic excitement he generated. The Shakers markedly increased their numbers as a result of revivalism; William Ellery Channing developed a Unitarian brand of Christian communism in opposition to revivalism; and under European influence there developed secular utopian schemes such as the Owenite and Fourierist experiments. Before looking closely at the way in which Noyes departed from the Wesleyan and Oberlin schools of Perfectionism, it is important to see how Noyes's reformulation of Christian history was consistent with other earlier revolutionary innovations and instrumental in transcending the tension between religion and world.

History, Millennium, and Utopia

The ancient Greek and Judeo-Christian traditions are separated by different historical visions. For the Greeks, history was an endless succession of cycles, a cosmic oscillation defining the form and structure within which the rhythm of events was repeated. The Judeo-Christian tradition, however, gave the world an alternative vision of history as divine drama: the curtain rose with creation, the play divided into acts of supernatural intervention, and closed with the day of judgment. Within the Christian scheme, Tuveson describes the development of a historical mode, the "millenarian," which expected the physical return of Christ and the saints accompanied by a series of wonderful, or at least preternatural, occurrences.[3] The second historical mode, the "Augustinian," regarded these predictions as alle-

gorical and maintained a firm dichotomy between the orders of
heaven and earth. The Reformation introduced the "millennialist,"
or "progressive millennialist," framework in which a literal millennium was indeed expected. Its description was in many ways allegorical and nothing preternatural would be required to bring it about.
History itself, under divine guidance and the divinely inspired works
of man, would bring about the triumph of Christian principles. By
the nineteenth century, alongside the secular idea of progress grew a
Christian alternative. The defeat of Satan and the powers of darkness
would be accomplished through a process of progressive spiritual
struggle and social amelioration.

The succession of historical modalities, when placed within a
Mannheimian framework of "ideological" and "utopian" mentality, turns our attention to sacred histories as transcendent instrumen-
talities. The "utopian" mentality refers to states of mind in experience, thought, and practice that are oriented toward objects that do
not exist in the actual situation. Not every such transcendent state of
mind is utopian, only those that, as they pass over into conduct, tend
to shatter, either partially or wholly, the order of things prevailing at
the time.[4]

The Christian historical modes discussed by Tuveson are all "utopian" in this sense, but they forge different relations between the sacred and secular realms. The millenarian mode consists of occasional
intrusions of the heavenly order in the world. The Augustinian mode
saw the cities of God "descending" at the time of the destruction of
the world on the day of judgment. The millennialist mode seamlessly
weaves the heavenly and earthly order into the fabric of progressive
history. The "world" was no longer merely an earthly trial or waiting period. It became the locus of meaningful spiritual and benevolent activity. The Reformation had made man an adjunct to the Holy
Spirit, its worldly instrument. All three of these historical modes
share a common trait—the placing of the second coming of Christ in
the indefinite future. His return will mark the beginning of the apoca-
lyptic era; either in miraculous or allegorical terms, the revelation to
John will be fulfilled.

The conceptual scheme of history has been of fundamental importance to more idiosyncratic utopian sects. The Shakers, for example,
divided the history of the world into four "dispensations" or stages.
The first, the "Antideluvian" dispensation, was the most primitive.
God was conceived only as a remote Great Spirit. The "Mosaic" dis-

pensation was a lawbound, preparatory period for the third dispensation, that of the primitive Church. Christ revealed God to be the loving father of mankind, not the remote arbitrary God of the Jews, he enjoined virtues of celibacy, and he established the primitive Church as his "earthly Heaven." The dispensation of Ann Lee revealed God as the mother of mankind and announced the possibility of earthly salvation for all. This final dispensation was the culminating work, encompassing all the valid teachings of the previous eras and beginning the world-wide establishment of the Shaker Church as the only path to Salvation. Ann Lee had inaugurated the final state of human history. It was the task of her followers to resist contamination by the world and to spread her teachings until God's work was completed.[5]

John Humphrey Noyes's New Sacred History and the Doctrine of Perfect Holiness

The idea of "perfection" had been creeping into the thoughts of even the more conservative clergy. Nathaniel Taylor, under whom John Humphrey Noyes studied at Yale, seemed to be moving in that direction. New York Perfectionist leaders—James Latourette, John B. Foote, and Hiram Sheldon—emphasized the doctrine of perfection more than Wesley and were even willing to be called "Perfectionists," but they did not go much further than admitting the theoretical possibility of spiritual perfection tempered by the threat of backsliding and degeneration. For Noyes, spiritual perfection in this world had been made possible through the Second Coming, introduced by the destruction of the temple at Jerusalem and the judgment of the Jews in A.D. 70. Perfect holiness was not only practically attainable, it was secure. On February 20, 1834, Noyes was overwhelmed by an intense religious experience that purged his soul:

on my bed that night I received the baptism which I desired and expected. Three times in quick succession a stream of eternal love gushed through my heart and rolled back again to its source. "Joy unspeakable and full of glory" filled my soul. All fear and doubt and condemnation passed away. I knew that my heart was clean, and that the Father and the Son had come and made their abode.[6]

Noyes did not regard himself as perfect in the sense of not needing improvement or in being immune to criticism; his was a spiritual perfection of faith for: "one may be perfect in *holiness*, and yet imperfect in *experience*, and subject to *infirmity*. We mean by perfect holiness (using the expression in the lowest sense), simply that *purity of heart* which gives a good *conscience*."[7]

The first stage of perfect holiness was the deliverance of the heart at Christ's feet and the purging of the soul of its pollution. This was possible through a process of confession and forgiveness. One must clear away the rubbish of one's own works, repent manifest sins and supposed works of righteousness, and become righteous not by works, but by receiving grace. One must believe that the Gospel was fact, not proposal—that it was a proclamation from God and a statement of his reconciliation with man through the death of Jesus. The way was then clear for pure faith in the resurrection of Christ. Security of perfect holiness is the gift of God. The same power that disposes one to believe also secures. Perfection of faith was only the first step toward spiritual perfection. The new challenge lay in finding the discipline necessary for sanctification—the improvements and true good works needed to bring action into harmony with spiritual purity.

By itself, Noyes's Perfectionism could have been dismissed as a new twist to the Wesleyan legacy; eccentric no doubt, but probably of no lasting importance. But John Humphrey Noyes's Perfectionism had at its core a radical reinterpretation of Christian history and Scripture that propelled him and his followers into utopia.

The contemporary world was so dissimilar to the heavenly kingdom that mere reform was inadequate. The institutions that were appropriate for restraint of the spiritually deficient were anachronistic anchors keeping humanity from rising to perfection. Perfect holiness could be nurtured only in a social, political, and economic contest patterned after the kingdom of heaven. The promised prophetic fulfillment gave Noyes the license for the extensive social and institutional innovations that the kingdom of heaven on earth required; "heavenly" institutions on earth would tap humankind's spiritual potential, resolving the tension between religion and world.

Noyes had shattered the religious orthodoxies that had established and legitimated the relationship between humanity and God, and mediated religion and world. By disconfirming the conventional religiohistoric scheme that located humankind in the cosmic design, Noyes burst the ideological constraints that bound the second Great Awakening leaders to moral reform and the institutional status quo.

Perfectionism offered a new worldview that legitimated radical social and institutional change. Law, economy, and sex, marriage, and the family were the immediate targets for inspired social change.

The New Covenant, and Freedom from Law and Political Order

Each stage of human development was associated with a specific relationship between God and man. Under the Jewish dispensation, Moses was the principal mediator between God and man, and the Mosaic code was the legal/ethical "contract" consonant with the Jewish covenant. Moses suffered under the burden of office and, according to Noyes, longed for a universal system of personal instruction from God. His longing for a new covenant was fulfilled in Jesus. Heaven and earth met and were one in Jesus, and the new covenant could dispense with law, for it would be etched in the heart.[8]

Formal religious law, like the Mosaic code, was a vestige of a previous religious state, unnecessary for purified man and inappropriate for the coming kingdom of heaven. Legality was an intolerable burden because it interfered with the sympathetic relationship between God and man. The Jews were bound to legal obedience. The faith of the Gospel and the new covenant frees the true Christian from the law. Like a cage, the law only contained, it did not train. It kept man within the reach of God's influence but it did not purify. The Gospel surpassed the law. Once man's heart was pure, external restraints were not only superfluous, they were obstacles to the advent of the heavenly order on earth.

The secular order should also be reevaluated if it violated God's law and obstructed the spiritual development of humanity. In this spirit, John Humphrey Noyes declared his independence from the government of the United States:

When I wish to form a true conception of the government of the United States, (using a personified representation) I picture to myself a bloated, swaggering libertine, trampling on the Bible—its own Constitution—its treaties with the Indians—the petitions of its citizens; with one hand whipping a Negro, tied to a liberty-pole, and with the other dashing an emaciated Indian to the ground.... But every other country is under the same reprobate authority. I must, then, either go out of the world, or find some way to live where I am, without being a hypocrite, or a partaker in the sins of the nation.[9]

Notwithstanding this harsh critique of the government, Noyes believed that democracy held promise for the kingdom of heaven on earth. What was lacking in our political system was universally acclaimed inspiration. Although the universe was not ruled democratically, the kingdom of heaven on earth would require administration, hence a political order. But this political order would not reflect the collective will of the masses, but the collective affirmation of inspiration. Leaders and their policies would be "elected" and formulated through divinely inspired acclamation. This political order, which Noyes called "democratic theocracy," sought to meld the universalism of regenerate souls with the elitism of spiritual virtuosity.[10]

Reliance on infallible inspiration and freedom from law, convention, and religious dogma were outgrowths of Noyes's doctrine of perfection and his new sacred history, and they freed him intellectually from worldly restraints in the transformation of social relations necessary for the kingdom of heaven on earth. This was particularly central to his economic and social-sexual theory.

Perfectionism and Economy

The religious basis of the Puritan vocation had done more than develop Christian discipline, duty, and character; it had created affluence and contributed to the creation of a dynamic economic system. But private property, self-seeking, and materialism were also byproducts of hard, disciplined work in a calling. These unanticipated consequences of religious belief were formidable obstacles to unselfish love of God, universal brotherhood, and the Christian equality of regenerate souls. Preparation for the kingdom of heaven on earth required sweeping aside the values and institutions that stood in the way of the heavenly order. Capitalism and private property would have to be replaced with an economic system modeled after the communism of the primitive Church.

We find references to communism throughout Noyes's writings, and in his later works he more frequently speaks of socialism. Though he makes no formal analytical distinction between them, he does seem to use "socialism" more often in reference to nonreligious communal experiments, reserving "communism" for religious communities. In his later work, *The History of American Socialism*, and the periodical the *American Socialist*, "communism" seems to be used as the religious subspecies of "socialism."[11] Though Noyes never mentioned Karl Marx directly, one can speculate that he hesitated to use the term "communism" when it began to be widely associated with a social theory that explicitly rejected religion.

Communism and religion were inseparable in Noyes's mind and he felt that it was only recently that they had grown apart. Their separation in the modern world was artificial:

The Revivalists had for their great idea the regeneration of the soul. The great idea of the Socialists was the regeneration of society, which is the soul's environment. These ideas belong together, and are the complements of each other. Neither can be successfully embodied by men whose minds are not wide enough to accept them both....

... The Revivalists failed for want of regeneration of society, and the Socialists failed for want of regeneration of the heart.[12]

Religion was the key to communism's success, and that is what separated the long-lasting and prosperous sectarian communities from the short-lived, bankrupt, or abandoned Owenite, Fourierist, and like-minded attempts. Earnest men of one religious faith were more likely to be respectful of organized authority and one another. In short, religion made people better fit for association.

Perfectionism, Love, Marriage, and the Family

Communism was not to be limited to mere property relations. Exclusive love, marriage, and family, no less than private property, stood in the way of unselfishness and universal love of God and man. Monogamous marriage was a legal contrivance of an earlier era of religious discipline reflecting society's sexual ambivalence and preventing humanity from fully enjoying God's finest gifts—the capacity for pleasure and the spiritual energy derived from sexual gratifications. According to Noyes, Paul counseled the primitive Church to love one another en masse, not in pairs, for exclusive love was absent in the kingdom of heaven.

The fellowship between Adam and Eve was, in Noyes's mind, open, fearless, and spiritual. With the original sin they were at once alienated from God and from each other. It was the task of the primitive Church to resolve the first alienation: the ecclesiastical system was broken up, the true religion was established, and full communication with God was renewed. It was the task of the Oneida Community, as the spiritual heir to the primitive Church, to break up the social system, establish the true external order, and reconcile the sexes.

Conventional love was comparable to the bondage of slavery, the degradation of narcotics, and the sinfulness of idolatry. True love "produces a true vibration with no bad effects or painful reaction following. It warms our hearts in such a way, that joy, health, and eternal life are its sequelae."[13]

Love meant, above all, contact with the creator. It must rise above individualism and selfishness and reach for universalism. "Anything short of this, any love of pleasure which stops in forms and individualities, and fails to pursue it up to the universal, is blind."[14] Selfishness represented that which looked upon men as separate, isolated beings, distant from God and fellowmen. This was the condition of the world at the time. The next step was the "true position of mankind": union with God and with each other.[15]

Noyes's ideas on exclusive love and marriage were first publicized when a private letter to one of his followers fell into the hands of Theophilus R. Gates, a radical Perfectionist and publisher of the newspaper the *Battle Axe and Weapons of War*. A letter written in confidence, intended only for the eyes of sympathizers, thrust Noyes into public controversy when Gates published it anonymously in an August 1837 edition of the *Battle Axe*. The following extract includes its main points:

I call a certain woman my wife—she is yours, she is Christ's and in him she is the bride of all saints. She is dear in the hands of a stranger, and according to my promise to her, I rejoice. My claim on her directly cuts across the marriage vows of this world and God knows the end.

... When the will of God is done on the earth as it is in heaven, *there will be no more marriage*. The marriage supper of the Lamb is a feast at which *every dish is free to every guest*. Exclusiveness, jealousy, quarreling, have no place there; for the same reason as that which forbids the guest at a thanksgiving dinner to claim each his separate dish and quarrel with the rest for this right. In a holy community there is no more reason why sexual intercourse would be restrained by law than why eating and drinking should be—and there is as little occasion for shame in the one case as in the other.[16]

Though Noyes regretted the letter's early publication, he openly admitted authorship and publicly defended his views. The uproar that followed caused a sensation among Perfectionists and many of his followers dropped away, leaving Noyes with a small but dedicated circle.

Immediate abandonment of marriage on a wide scale was not advocated by Noyes, for the world was still spiritually immature. Plunging unregenerate humanity into the social relations of the kingdom of heaven would only lead to immorality and licentiousness, as the various "free love" sects demonstrated. Once secure spiritual perfection was recognized as attainable in this world, and once the individual underwent an intense religious experience in which the heart was cleansed by Jesus, there was no need to fear the immorality and licentiousness that haunted the unregenerate. Living on a higher religious plane, sexual, marital, and familial convention could be discarded for the heavenly amative order. This was justified by Noyes's radical reorientation of Christian history. After the Second Coming, the door to mortal spiritual perfection, which had been closed since the Fall, had been reopened and sexual life no longer needed to be mediated by law or custom.

In the early summer of 1846, Noyes judged that a small coterie within the community at Putney was sufficiently advanced to abandon exclusive love and marriage. "Complex marriage," guided by the principle that none be exclusively bound in love or law and that all be "married" to all, was initiated by John Noyes and his wife, Harriet, and George Cragin and his spouse, Mary.[17]

Familial relations would also have to be altered, because they were expressions of exclusive love and emotional possessiveness. The love and emotional support expected of kin would have to be extended to the community in order to approach the unselfish love of the heavenly kingdom. On another level, Noyes found the family circumscribed by blood relations to be of primary importance in explaining private property, materialism, and personal attachment to wealth; and a fundamental obstacle to the communism of the primitive Church.

Accepted ideas about sex and gender roles were also abandoned along with conventional sexual, marital, and familial relations. In the kingdom of heaven on earth, men and women would realize their full potential. For women this meant a significant elevation in status. No longer would they be subject to the cultural restraints of women's "separate sphere" or torn by contradictions that raised them to saintly pedestals as defenders of religion and morals but kept them from bringing their angelic nature to bear on the world. Nor would they be subject to a Christian misogyny that portrayed them as temptresses responsible for the introduction of sin into the world.

For Noyes, God and humanity were dual in nature, composed of both male and female attributes. Assertiveness, daring, strength, and vitality defined masculinity; and demureness, spiritual refinement, and prudence were femininity's distinctive features. Noyes had no intentions of abandoning gender traits that his contemporaries considered God-ordained, or "natural"; nor did he wish to stretch women's separate sphere to confront a corrupt world with feminine Christian benevolence. Noyes saw the idealized features of masculinity and femininity distorted in worldly culture and society. Masculinity and femininity were complementary rather than antagonistic. In the kingdom of heaven on earth these estranged dimensions of personality and character would be reconciled in spiritually perfect men and women. In practical terms this required cultivating the characteristics of the opposite sex and maintaining them in proper balance with one's own sexual nature. The supermasculine male as well as the ultrafeminine female were not the archetypes of their sex, but aberrations who had tipped the scales of gender too far and were thus unable to realize their full human potential.

For John Humphrey Noyes and the Oneida Community, the theological leap into utopia was made with a brilliant reorganization of the Christian tradition that severed religious historical continuity and made spiritual and social perfection a worldly possibility. The tension between religion and world had been resolved on the ideological level. The world was not a trial, test, or way station before other-worldly salvation or damnation. The world was where the religious promise would be consummated. Freed from the anachronistic constraints of antedated religious law and social convention, the Oneida Community's practical task was to realize individual and collective spiritual perfection through mystical and ascetic discipline and the creation of social and cultural forms appropriate to the kingdom of heaven on earth.

7

The Oneida
Community: Tran-
scending the Tensions
between Religion and
World in Practice

With the declaration "the
kingdom of heaven has come," and the initiation of complex marriage on a limited scale, John Humphrey Noyes and his small circle of
followers at Putney, Vermont, were no longer just religious zealots
and eccentrics (which would have been by no means rare for the
time) but were rather threats to the civic and moral order. Rumors of
the "goings-on" at the Putney Community, reinforced by defectors
who "confessed" to their knowledge of complex marriage but had
not participated, raised the moral dander of the town. The state at-
torney general was alerted and presented the available evidence to
a grand jury. Noyes was arrested as an adulterer and released on a
$2,000 bond.

As local emotion escalated, the community decided that non-
natives of Putney should disperse temporarily, and the Noyeses and
Cragins planned to establish themselves in New York State. Joining
some New York Perfectionists at a former Indian reservation at
Oneida, New York, the Oneida Community began in Indian cabins
under spartan conditions. It is not necessary for my purposes to re-
count the full history of the Oneida Community; instead I will con-
centrate on its organization and its relationship to religion and
world.[1]

The Oneida Community was not formed to "call people away

from their homes and employments to tend to religion," but to turn "their very arrangements for getting a living into the essential conditions of a school and a church."[2] The distinction between religious and secular pursuits was abandoned, and the original members dressed all life in religious garb. With religion permeating all aspects of life there was little need of formal ritual or regular meetings for services or prayers. Sunday received no special attention and Christmas was scarcely recognized. For the Bible communists every day was sacred. February 20, the anniversary of the day in 1834 when John Humphrey Noyes received salvation from sin, was celebrated with quiet festivities—speeches, toasts to Perfectionism, and so on— and was followed by a dance and even an exchange of presents. By the 1860s it was celebrated with less formality and it is scarcely mentioned in the community newspapers of later years.

The early settlers who joined Noyes at Oneida were "neither poets nor political anarchists." They were young, hardy, and skilled in farming and the trades. Most came from rural areas and small towns in New York and New England. A number of the men were farmers, and printers, trapmakers, machinists, architects, shoemakers, and bookkeepers were represented. A few clerks, teachers, a lawyer, a Methodist minister, and a doctor rounded out a young, skilled, pious, and middle-class lot. The vast majority had been moved by revivalism. There is no information available on the religious affiliation of one-quarter of the original members but one-third were Congregationalists; one-fifth were Methodists; eleven were Baptists; five were Presbyterians; and there was one Dutch Reformist, Millerite, Unitarian, Quaker, Tobiasite, Universalist, and Free Churcher.[3]

There is no evidence to suggest these people were wandering truthseekers, flirting with one religious enthusiasm after another. The evidence does confirm their own evaluation, written in 1853: "The main body of those who have joined the Association at Oneida, are sober, substantial men and women, of good previous character, and position in society."[4] That the Oneida Community attracted the pious, serious, and established suggests that the religious questions faced by Noyesian Perfectionism were not the concerns of an eccentric fringe or of social and cultural extremists. The issues to which John Humphrey Noyes spoke occupied the hearts and minds of the hard working, the educated, and the respectable; and Noyes's revolutionary social-sexual, economic, and political innovations appealed to a group that had been, in many respects, rather conventional.

The Politics of Consensus

At the community's outset, Noyes's authority was as close to the charismatic ideal as conceivable, resting on claims to divine inspiration. Community members did not believe, nor were they led to believe, that Noyes was a new incarnation of Christ. They did believe him to be a link in a spiritual chain descending from God through Christ and Paul. Noyes regarded himself and was regarded by others as the instrument through which the Holy Spirit flowed to earth. The thought and example of John Humphrey Noyes was to be the measure of all things.

Though grounded in the person and thought of John Humphrey Noyes, the community's political organization strove for a consensual politics reminiscent of the Puritan town meeting. Matters of religion, business, and social relations were opened to collective "inspiration" guided by Noyes and affirmed by the community. True to the charismatic ideal, community leaders were not selected by ballot, but "elected" by divine acclamation. Inspiration did not involve hammering out theology, programs, and policy from differing parties in a democratic forum, but meant ascertaining where, among the contending ideas and ideals, inspiration lay. Noyes, as founder, spiritual shepherd, and conduit for the Holy Spirit, could be counted on to either provide "inspiration" or discover it when consensus was difficult or spoiled by stubborn holdouts.

In their *Principles of Association* (1848), the community forged a formal constitution or written compact and rules. "Inspiration," the care and admonition of those proved qualified to shepherd the group, and free criticism were found sufficient. After 1864 new members were asked to sign a statement speaking to the issue of community-held property and support in lieu of wages, as several disgruntled seceders had sued for back wages.[5]

Religious ideals were used to buttress democratic ideology from the very beginning of colonial political life in the New World. Well into the nineteenth century, Protestant thought has been clearly divided in the debate over democracy. Second Great Awakening Protestant political ambivalence was expressed in a spectrum that ranged from the democratic radicalism of Antimasonry to Tory-like Episcopalianism. Finney and Beecher locked horns over religious issues that had democratic ramifications, but revivalism's exclusive concern with the state of the individual soul diverted confrontations from political and economic institutions. The issue of slavery was the notable exception though the revivalist critique was moral rather than democratic. None of the major religious leaders of the day was able to overcome the conflict between religion and democracy, or the conflict within religion over democracy.

The Oneida Community, under the guidance of John Humphrey Noyes, sought to transcend the conflict over democracy by a "democratic theocracy" that sought to meld the universalism of regenerate souls with the elitism of spiritual virtuosity. In historical terms, democratic theocracy was a throwback to the Puritan "democracy" of the town meeting, and ran counter to secular political developments. In their own words, their government was democratic "in as much as the privilege of criticism is distributed through the whole body, and the power which it gives is accessible to any one who will take pains to attain Good judgment. It is Aristocratic, in as much as the best critics have the most power. It is Theocratic, in as much as the Spirit of Truth alone can give the power of genuine criticism."[6]

Although democracy was praised as the form of worldly government best suited to the spirit of the Bible, it was still an earthly order, hence only temporary and transitional. It is the "midway and milestone of the journey" from monarchical and despotic government to the kingdom of God. We are reminded that the universe is not ruled by a democratically elected official, but by an absolute monarch. Not democracy but the kingdom of God is the elevation of mankind.[7]

In 1844 Noyes admitted that even with the advent of the kingdom of heaven on earth the nation would still require a human form of political order to govern municipal affairs. Democracy, best suited to the spirit of the Bible and the policy of Jesus Christ, would require a theocratic element in government that was spiritual and didactic rather than legislative. This theocratic element would be at work in the whole people and would indirectly determine legislation. Through its influence, the voice of God would reverberate in the voice of the people. Instead of legislation by representative, Noyes advocated a kind of national town meeting in which a periodical paper established at the seat of government would be the forum where laws were proposed, discussed, enacted, and recorded. The executive function of government would remain untouched.[8]

Although democracy was considered the true complement to theocracy, the democratic elements of the Oneida Community could only seem superficial to outside observers. No one joined the community without recognizing Noyes as Christ's representative on earth and his divinely sanctioned and inspired absolute power. At the helm of an inspired theocracy, Noyes ruled as an autocrat with a light hand, leaving the application of his general principles to his lieutenants and the community at large. Ascending fellowship, the pattern of sexual relations that reflected the community's spiritual pecking order and governed complex marriage, established a hierarchy of social/spiritual prestige. With authority, privilege, and power varying with propinquity to Noyes and his inner circle, the free and public exchange of ideas and disagreements over policy characteristic of democracy often gave way to deference and quiet consent.[9]

The evening meetings and mutual criticism were the social arrangements that sublimated the tension between democracy and religious absolutism. At its peak, 253 members resided at Oneida and all were expected to attend the evening meeting. "Partly social, partly intellectual, partly industrial and partly religious in character," it was the centerpiece of community life.[10] Assembled in the large public room in the Mansion House, the Bible communists listened to community correspondence and articles from community and outside publications, and they participated in discussions of all community matters, mutual criticism, and religious subjects. There was no regular preaching but often one of Noyes's "home-talks" was read aloud, by Noyes in person if he was at Oneida. As business expanded new orders were announced and applauded, policy discussed, and changes in shop methods considered.

The evening meetings were often dominated by the more articulate members. All who had something to say were encouraged, but women scarcely participated. Most were content to listen while sewing, knitting, and quilting. Regardless of the topic discussed, consensus was the ideal and practical goal of the meeting. In this respect the meetings were similar to the Massachusetts town meetings of an earlier era. Noyes and the central members brought issues before the community, they were openly discussed, and differences of opinion and reservations were respected, but when it was time for a decision to be made, unanimity was expected. Most often the majority merely ratified the proposals of the central members. If serious objections to any measure surfaced, action was delayed until the objections were removed or worked out. Noyes insisted that "the majority never go ahead leaving a grumbling minority behind."[11] On important business and social issues Noyes's opinion could be counted on to hold sway. If Noyes was away from the community, as was often the case because he regularly visited branch communities and Perfectionist sympathizers, he was consulted by mail. Since Noyes was recognized as divinely inspired and Christ's representative, defiance would have meant more than just disagreement on a single point: it would be tantamount to rejecting Christ and the community's reason for being.

Noyes imported mutual criticism from Andover Theological Seminary—where it was instituted among a secret society of students ("The Brethren") who had pledged to go on foreign missions—and it became the cornerstone of community life at Oneida. The object of mutual criticism was

not to irritate by constant fault-finding, but to present to each one from time to time, as a mirror, the *tout ensemble*, the whole of his character, as it is seen by those around him—the aim being not only to point out the way of specific improvement, but also to produce humility and softness of heart, in which all good things grow and all bad things die.[12]

Purity of heart was only the first step on the road to perfect holiness. Criticism provided an external measure of one's religious and social achievement and an index of the virtues and flaws that one thought hidden, overcome, or obvious. Spiritual as well as social qualities and work habits were fit for criticism. Defects consisted of such things as stubbornness, self-centeredness and egotism, a tendency toward fanaticism or excitement, impulsiveness, a domineering or overly submissive character, excessive "manliness," "femininity," or vanity, and imprudence. Merits were such things as harmony in conversation, "a good heart," intelligence, loyalty, unselfishness, and other spiritual values. These defects and merits were staples for the critical appetites of the community. Love, respect, sincerity, patience, meekness, and charity were expected of the critic. If the subject could take pleasure in the positive accomplishments, remain calm, self-possessed, and patient, and side with the truth and justice of criticism, he or she would endure and profit from its most severe barbs.

A standing committee, selected by the community and changed every three months, was created to organize criticism and allow everyone the opportunity to serve as critics as well as subjects. In the great majority of cases criticism was freely solicited by subjects, but all were expected to "volunteer." Criticism was sometimes by the entire "family," the standing committee, or a group of six, eight, twelve, or more selected by the subject from those best acquainted with him or her. When it was noticed that a community member was suffering from faults and might benefit, they were "invited" to submit to criticism. Extreme cases of disobedience to community regulations or "obsession by influences averse to general harmony" prompted criticism by the community or its leaders without solicitation.

To be more than just superficial, censorious, back-biting, or flattering, criticism had to be artfully developed:

It studies character as a painter would a picture, exploring and analyzing the whole. It refers actions back to their hidden spring—traces excesses to some virtue which is overstrained—points out the deficiencies which indicate the want of union with life of an opposite nature—is healthy, yet temperate in awarding praise and blame, and leaves its subjects neither flattered nor despairing, but earnest and hopeful.[13]

It was felt best for the subject to sit silently during criticism, accepting the sincerity, love, and truthfulness of the critics. Afterwards, the subject generally acknowledged the faults of character exposed and thanked the critics for the justice of their comments and their recommendations for improvement. A thorough criticism by the more skilled and perceptive members could be a shattering experience, a deflation of ego by the baring of poorly hidden or unrealized flaws and pompous self-righteousness. Criticism at the hands of Noyes himself was akin to a Virgilian tour of one's soul. Subjects emerged from criticism visibly shaken and humbled. After the personal meditation and reevaluation of self that followed, most members came to regard their criticism as cathartic, a renewal of their faith in God, the community, Noyes, and their own progressive improvement.

Criticism was, in fact, the community's main instrument of social control. Through its agency the practical elements of Perfectionism were elucidated, deviance reprimanded, and congeniality and conformity rewarded. Personal programs for spiritual, social, intellectual, and occupational improvements were suggested. Even those subject to the severest criticism could take heart in the outflow of community concern and their confidence that improvement was within reach. There were members who would not or could not conform to community life, even after repeated criticisms, and seceded voluntarily. I know of only one exception in which a recalcitrant member was literally tossed out the front door.

Criticism was also used in healing, because it was believed that the weakest spot in one's character and conduct provided access to disease. When criticism was rendered sincerely it threw the subject into a sweat, bringing on a reaction of life against disease—breaking fever, illness, and debility and restoring health. When many were stricken by a diptheria epidemic in 1863 and several members died, criticism was enlisted to rout the disease and many successes were claimed.

Historical criticism carried the method into the members' past, for "we are what our past lives have made us." Half-forgotten past wrongs and secrets were "darkening and poisonous to present experience," and confession and criticism lifted their weight from the spirit.[14]

Every facet of community life, from criticism and finance to haircuts and recreation, fell under the domain of one of the twenty-one standing committees. The administration of all the various economic, publishing, and social duties was divided among forty-eight additional departments. This may seem a ponderous division of labor and authority for a community that had 253 members at its largest. In practice it was an efficient organization yielding exceptional commitment. The sheer number of committees offered every member a responsible position and infused diligence and enthusiasm into even the most menial task. Rotation of committee and department appointments and labor—except for positions that required special skills and technical abilities—satisfied those doing disagreeable work, made for variety and interest, and prevented the formation of exclusive fiefdoms. Personal tastes, ability, and contentment, as well as community needs, were considered in all appointments to labor.

The "Business Board," consisting of the heads of all departments and any other member who wished to attend, met every Sunday morning. The business of the past week was discussed and new action planned. At the Sunday evening meeting the board secretary's report was read to all and discussed. Whatever received general or unanimous approval was carried out. Once a year, at a special board meeting, the plans for the following year were mapped out in detail. As a matter of principle nothing was attempted without the general consent of the community. When a proposal met with objections, the matter was shelved for further discussion.

The new covenant and era of the kingdom of heaven on earth required stepping beyond worldly political order. Religious belief and inspiration could no longer be viewed as supporting or opposing popular will; it had to shape popular will itself. The evening meeting, mutual criticism, and the committee system provided the democratic trappings to Noyes's democratic theocracy and offered the opportunity for collective affirmation of Perfectionist beliefs and the inspiration of community leadership so vital to community commitment. Discussion, disagreement, and participation were encouraged from the most important social and financial affairs to the most mundane matters, but decision making required unanimity. Harmony and consensus were the index of inspiration. Suggestions meeting with dissent were either withdrawn, reworked, or discussed until general approval or rejection was achieved. Those who persisted in opposition to the general will would certainly be criticized for their stubbornness, selfishness, and inharmonious spirit.

The charismatic leadership of Noyes assured unanimity for his major decisions. Any issue that Noyes threw his full weight behind was offered to the community for affirmation rather than critical discussion. Majority rule can never sustain charismatic inspiration, but the Oneida variant of charismatic authority that allowed for seemingly active participation and acclamation appeared to sustain democratic forms without the contradictions becoming problematic. This politics of consensus, guided by inspiration and Noyes's special status as worldly leader and heavenly agent, grounded the community's organizational and social innovations in a legitimacy structure that resolved the tension between theology and secular democratic developments. The democracy of the Puritan town meeting was renovated in a transcendent utopian context in which religion and world had been theoretically unified.

Transcending the Tension between Religion and Sexuality

The possibility of introducing the heavenly order on earth, coupled with the freedom from law and legality provided by the new covenant, called for new sexual and familial relations and made the resolution of nineteenth-century sexual ambivalence possible. Opposing assertions of the inherent danger of sex as a threat to piety and health —if carried to "lustful" extremes—and the claim that sex was natural and healthy could be transcended by a religious justification. Sexual desire, expression, and gratification were not based in evil, nor were they temptations to sinfulness and irreligion or merely normal biological needs; they were a divine gift—the instrument for unselfish universal love and communion with God. As the vanguard of the kingdom of heaven on earth, John Humphrey Noyes and the Oneida

Community were granted the license to initiate a system of sexual-familial relations that would realize the promise of true love, sexual ecstasy, and true family order. Sexuality could still be lustful, but collective norms and mores arising from their religious beliefs made sex at Oneida a communal reaffirmation of unselfishness and universal love rather than asocial exclusiveness and possessiveness. Gratification of individual and conjugal needs were insufficient; sex had to affirm collective affections and love of God.

Weber noted that sexual ecstasy, the fusion of souls in passion, may be interpreted symbolically as a sacrament and, in that respect, may be equivalent to a mystical experience. This inner-worldly "earthly sensation of salvation by mature love competes in the sharpest possible way with the devotion of a supra-mundane God, with the devotion of an ethically rational order of God, or with the devotion of a mystical bursting of individuation, which alone appear "genuine" to the ethic of brotherhood."[15]

The substitution of sexual for religious sacrament and the other possible points of conflict between religion, God, and erotic pleasure were transcended in complex marriage. Erotic ecstasy was not an alternative or substitute for religion, but a mystical and ascetic experience, a communion with God and community through one's lover; the self-conscious control of base physical nature; and the elevation of spiritual nature in male continence and ascending fellowship. Spiritual perfection was used to purge any doubts or lingering feelings of sin, for their salvation was secured by God-given purity of heart. Sin could only be the result of a conscious, premeditated violation of Perfectionist values and order. The weakness of the flesh was normal and mortal, and could be overcome by progressive religious discipline.

Later, we shall see that the community's transcendence of the tension between religion and the erotic sphere and family was not effective in the long run. The conflict between religion and sexuality re-emerged on a different level, over the administration of community sexual life.

Sex, Love, and Marriage at Oneida

Replacement of the conventional marriage arrangement with a system more consonant with Christian ideals was Paul's explicit message and Noyes's practical task. Romantic love degenerates into "ownership" in marriage. A man is given the right to demand love and services from his spouse regardless of his conduct or worthiness. The wife is looked upon as an object, owned and used for pleasure. The tendency to excessive and idolatrous commitment to family was fueled by marriage, leaving little time or energy for God and improvement. Based on exclusiveness, marriage binds couples for life though there is no reason to suppose that this is natural or desirable. The permanence and exclusiveness of marriage, concluded Noyes, is responsible for many unnecessary evils; it provokes "secret adultery" in acts or heart; binds unmatched and sunders matched natures; makes scanty and monotonous allowances for the sexual appetite, producing poverty and contraction of taste, stinginess, and jealousy; and makes no provision for puberty, when the sexual appetite is strongest and the individual most tempted to licentiousness and other sexual perversions. Finally, conventional marriage makes it impossible to employ scientific breeding to improve the human race.[16] The Oneida Community had to attack all these problems to achieve individual and collective perfection.

Marriage, as it was then practiced, was an insurmountable obstacle to the true Christian life. Love of God and one's neighbor took a second seat to familial selfishness: a better way was implied by Paul's dictum, "In the resurrection they neither marry nor are given in marriage." Exclusive, selfish, invidious marriage must be replaced by an inclusive arrangement, embracing all in unselfish, open, fulfilling love on a grand scale. In this spirit the Oneida Community announced they had:

left the simple form of marriage and advanced to the complex stage of it. We have no quarrel with those who believe in exclusive dual marriage and faithfully observe it, but we have concluded that for us there is a better way. The honor and faithfulness that constitute an ideal marriage may exist between two hundred as well as two: while the guarantees for women and children are much greater in the Community than can be had in any private family. The results of the complex system we may sum up by saying that men are rendered more courteous, women more winning, children are better born, and both sexes are personally free.[17]

In short, Noyes saw no intrinsic difference between property in things or persons. "Amativeness and acquisitiveness are only different channels of the same stream." Selfishness and exclusiveness in material and social-sexual relations alike alienated the individual from God and man.[18]

Sex and Spiritual Perfection: The Oneida Sexual Economy

The Oneida Community considered sex the paramount sensual experience and the most spiritually elevating. It is intercourse between human life, and all other sensual pleasures fall short on this count because they involve either inanimate matter or "inferior" life forms. The melting of egotism in sexual intercourse is the ecstasy of true communion, for selfhood is dissolved in love. The transcendent experience of sexual ecstasy merges "I" with "thou" and both with God, the ultimate source of pleasure and spiritual growth.[19] As God's gift, sex is natural and should be shameless and guiltless. As a sacrament and source of spiritual growth, sex must be bound by good faith. Its danger lies in selfishness, lovelessness, exclusiveness, and repression.

The system of complex marriage was initiated on a limited scale at Putney and brought to Oneida on a community-wide basis. Originally the female was approached directly by the male and was free to accept or decline his advances. By 1860, the request was made through a third party, usually an older woman or a central member of the community. The function of the intermediary was to preserve the woman from embarrassment, check on members' activities, and record all encounters. Documenting sexual activity enabled the community to guard against exclusive relationships and guarantee adherence to the principles of "ascending fellowship."

The Oneida sexual economy was organized around ascending fellowship and recognized differences of individual spiritual development. Sex produced spiritual power, energy, and magnetism. Association with those further along on the path to perfection, reasoned Noyes, would increase one's own spiritual "capital." Young members were encouraged to forge liaisons with older, spiritually mature partners—ascending fellowship—and older members were responsible for drawing fellowship upward. Descending fellowship drew the individual of superior spirituality downward. Unfortunately ascending fellowship could not be had without the other partner suffering from descending fellowship. Ascending fellowship was always in order and need not be limited. Descending fellowship, however, held the danger of excessively tapping one's spiritual resources and was expected to be limited by the need for recharging ascending fellowship. One must be prepared to limit oneself when spiritual resources were being excessively depleted, and seek out partners to restore one's assets.

Noyes and the Oneida Community also recognized "horizontal fellowship," friendship between spiritual equals. Horizontal liaisons contributed little toward spiritual development and tended toward degeneration and deterioration but were not completely repudiated. Though development and progress required ascending fellowship, the exclusion of descending fellowships smacked of selfishness and was criticized as strongly as exclusively descending relations.[20] Sexual activity and adherence to community principles were further regulated by the community's fundamental instrument of social control, mutual criticism.

Oneida Community's sexual economy went beyond the choice of partners to the act itself. Noyes isolated two separate sexual processes: the amative and the propagative. A proper balance between them was required to save individuals from "bankruptcy." Amativeness, the emotional component of sexual love, was "profitable," it kept the "capital of life" circulating between the partners; the propagative component was "expensive," transmitting energy to a third party. Ejaculation drained a man's vitality and led to disease. Conception was even more costly. Pregnancy, the agonies of childbirth, and the cares of nursing levied a heavy tax on the vitality of women, and the burden of child rearing exacted a heavy toll on both parents. Shakerism was rejected as shutting off "profit" as well as "expenses," and Robert Dale Owen's "moral physiology"—limiting procreation and restraining sex by coitus interruptus—was unnatural and wasteful. The proper solution was "male continence."[21]

Control was the linchpin of Noyes's sexual economy and he divided intercourse into a series of processes that were under the male's control until a point just prior to ejaculation:

The sexual conjunction of male and female no more necessarily involves the discharge of semen than of the urine. The discharge of the semen, instead of being the main act of sexual intercourse, properly so called, is really the sequel and termination of it. Sexual intercourse, pure and simple, is the conjunction of the organs of union, and the interchange of magnetic influences, or conversation of spirits, through a medium of that conjunction.[22]

Just as a rower paddling downstream toward a waterfall must know the point of no return, a man must learn the point after which he loses control.

Noyes's interest in continence stemmed from his own married life. In the course of six years his wife Harriet suffered five painful births, from which only one baby survived. After their last disappointment he pledged he would never again expose his wife to such fruitless suffering. His first solution was abstention, followed later by male continence. The method, said Noyes, was natural, healthy, and "favorable to amativeness," for it vastly increased sexual pleasure for both partners and could be sustained for any length of time without satiety or exhaustion. It opened the way for scientific, well-ordered procreation and it was effective and easy to learn.[23]

The practical consequences of such a system in a community that accepted sex as natural, as neither a creatural wickedness nor a residue of the Fall, was an effective means of birth control. Between 1848 and 1869 forty-four children were born in the community. Eight of these were conceived before the parents joined the community, and at least five were sanctioned by the community. At most, thirty-one children were accidentally conceived over a period of twenty-one years in a population that reached 217 members who were over twenty-one years old by 1871.[24] "Accidents" led to curtailed encounters. The male's choice was self-control, the threat of public disapproval in mutual criticism, or private rejection.

The next step in complex marriage was a program of eugenics that was initiated as "stirpiculture" in 1869. Its goal was scientific procreation to create a genetic stock predisposed to the religious, intellectual, and physical requirements of spiritual perfection. A resolution was signed by all women of childbearing age to the effect that they did not belong to themselves in any respect, that they belonged first to God and second to John Humphrey Noyes as God's true representative. The declaration further stated that they had no rights or personal feelings in regard to childbearing that would in the least embarrass or oppose him in his choice of scientific combination. They agreed to put aside all envy, childishness, and self-seeking, and to rejoice with those who are the chosen candidates. They would, if necessary, become martyrs to science and cheerfully resign all desire to become mothers if for any reason Noyes deemed them unfit for propagation. Above all, they offered themselves as "living sacrifices" to God and true communism. Thirty-eight young men of the community signed a similar statement.[25]

Most participants selected their own mates and applied as a couple, one-fourth of all stirpiculture unions were actually suggested by the stirpiculture committee. As a consequence of ascending fellowship, the older men were usually higher in spirituality and more likely to be chosen as fathers. Stirpiculture and the limits imposed by ascending fellowship became, as we shall see, a considerable source of resentment and internal conflict.

There were several drawbacks to the complex marriage system. Couples frequently fell in love and this led to criticism of those who failed to suppress exclusive attachments. The couple that desired sex was originally allowed to remain together all night. This practice was later forbidden due to the exhausting effects of long continued intercourse if a man was particularly effective in continence, and in order to prevent the long private conversations that might have led to exclusive love. Persistent exclusive attachment could lead to suspension of sexual privileges, or the offending couple would be considered less spiritual and their choice of partners limited. As a last resort, one of the offending pair could be sent to the branch community at Wallingford, Connecticut, until the infatuation had been overcome. Usually the system of ascending fellowship prevented a young man and a young woman from having a sexual relationship. It is not known whether the men were dissatisfied with continence. The few males who have written on the subject after the breakup left favorable accounts of the practice.

An impressive amount of public relations was necessary to prevent the Oneida Community from coming to the same end as the Putney experiment. Noyes and the Oneida Community were continually refuting local and clerical accusations of licentiousness. If the community had remained closed to outside eyes it would have been impossible to defend. The Bible communists accommodated thousands of visitors yearly, providing food and lodging, guided tours, and entertainment. Visitors could not fail to validate the community claim that:

a just scrutiny of the household habits of the Oneida Community during any period of its history would not show a licentious spirit, but the opposite of licentiousness. It would disclose less careless familiarity of the sexes—less approach to anything like "bacchanalian" revelry—vastly less unregulated speech and conduct—than is found in an equal circle of what is called good society in the world.[26]

Regardless of what outsiders imagined, the community claimed a strong tendency toward sexual abstinence and reserve.

There is no doubt that the Oneida Community's image of respectability was further enhanced by its unassailable reputation for hon-

esty and fairness in trade, employment practices, and its contribution
to the local economy.

The Status of Women at the Oneida Community

Women in the outside world, proclaimed Noyes, were no freer than
slaves. Prisoners of often loveless marriages, chattellike nonentities
submissive to the sexual demands of their spouses, often physically
debilitated by repeated childbirths, they were condemned to a life as
household drudges. At Oneida, women were to be freed from possessiveness, compulsory sex and childbirth, and the restraints of sex-
determined occupational roles. No man had the right to demand the
love of a woman, claim sexual privileges, or fertilize a woman without her consent.

Like most of his contemporaries, Noyes recognized "natural" personality traits associated with sexual differentiation. But these traits
were not mutually exclusive: God was dual, made up of male and female elements, and humanity was made in his image. It was the duty
of each community member to cultivate the complementary characteristics of the opposite sex. The Oneida Community did not reject
the prevailing notion of sexual character, they elevated the female
nature. Femininity was not seen as a weakness; it was a virtue, not
only in women but also in men. A proper balance of masculinity and
femininity in men and women was the ideal.

Under the Oneida system of Bible communism women achieved
much of the status for which the women's rights movement was cam-
paigning. They were free to decline the sexual advances of any community member and free to choose a sexual partner. All occupations,
including leadership, were open to female members, should they
acquire the requisite skill. There also was no discrimination by sex as
the basis for training. Men and women worked side by side in many
community industries and it was found that mingling at work made
their labor more attractive and enjoyable. Household labor, particularly kitchen work, was done by women more often than men but
this practive rarely raised contention: job rotation and training in
other skills were available for the dissatisfied. Those who, in the long
run, remained in "female" occupations, such as kitchen work and
child care, claimed to genuinely enjoy the work and found satisfaction in their contribution to the life-style and well-being of the
community.

Though elevated, the status of women at the Oneida Community fell short of equality. Differences in temperament were God-ordained. The community opposed the women's rights movement not because they did not agree with its portrait of injustice and deprivation of liberty, but because of the fashion in which the movement sought dignity: by setting themselves in opposition to men and by relinquishing their feminine roles. By "playing" men, they ran contrary to heavenly organization. This misguided approach would lead to confusion, despair, and the destruction of feminine nature and the dual nature of humankind.[27]

Communism was the best hope for woman for through it she would be spiritually and socially elevated in consonance with her natural traits, and she would be fulfilled in her God-ordained place alongside, yet in service to, men, because Community women "have not ceased to love and honor the truth that 'man is the head of woman,' and that woman's highest God-given right is to be 'the glory of man.' "[28]

Though members occasionally complained that women were far too quiet at evening meetings when weighty matters of business and policy were discussed, women were involved in all phases of community operations, and their roles included editorial work with community publications and leadership of the numerous committees that oversaw operations. No evidence has come to light to suggest that Community women felt deprived of freedom, dignity, and opportunity.

Children at the Oneida Community

Children provided a sticky emotional problem for the Oneida Community. Parents were not discouraged from warm emotional attachments with their children but they were warned of the tendency of such relationships to degenerate into possessiveness, selfishness, and exclusivity. Of all the forms of love open to man, that between parent and child is, cautioned Noyes, the least spiritual and beneficial—yet it is this form of love to which men and women are most attracted. Love of children was a descending fellowship of the most dangerous sort, for excessive love toward a child dulled the adults' appetite for ascending fellowship.[29]

The social and religious nature of complex marriage required collective child rearing in order to protect parents from monopolizing descending fellowships and exclusive, possessive attachments, and to save the children from developing these spiritual handicaps. The community reserved a wing of their Mansion House for the housing, education, and recreation of its children. Infants stayed with their mothers until they were weaned. Once separated from their mothers, infants were collectively tended in the children's wing by community members who seemed especially gifted in child care and education. As they grew older, children "graduated" into peer groupings with their cohorts that represented their level of education, responsibility, and freedom.

Segregated but not isolated, community children did not want for adult attention or affection. Warm, loving relationships between biological parents and offspring and between children and other adults were encouraged as long as they did not become exclusive or "sticky." Regular private visits were allowed between parents and children. Pierrepont Noyes's chronicle of an Oneida boyhood suggests that parent-child relationships were generally loving and affectionate, but that private visits had an emotional urgency foreign to conventional family structures:

The Community system was harder on mothers than on their children. Whenever I was permitted to visit my mother in her mansard room—once or twice a week (I have forgotten which)—she always seemed trying to make up for lost opportunity, lavishing affection on me until, much as I loved her, I half grudged the time taken from play with those toys which she had—I think somewhat surreptitiously—collected for my visits.[30]

If either adult or child exhibited "stickiness" it would be noted in criticism, or private visits would be curtailed until those feelings were controlled. Pierrepont Noyes's memoirs expose an ambivalence that must have shadowed all strong emotional relationships within the community; love and affectionate contact were enjoyed, yet could generate guilt and reproof.

In child rearing particular attention was paid to the cultivation of obedience, and our chronicler recalls punishment, even rare "whippings," being justified and fair. Although each child was theoretically the charge of all adults, the teachers and supervisors of the children's wing were the primary disciplinarians. In Pierrepont Noyes's day, discipline was meted out by William "Papa" Kelley who, in young "Pip's" eyes, seemed to be the custodian of that salvation that was the special asset of the community. Kelley was recognized as the plenary representative of John Humphrey Noyes (Pierrepont's biological father), who he knew dealt directly with the heavenly agencies of salvation. "Never, in their [adult] contacts with the children, was there any suggestion of uncertain standards of conduct or any compromise with wrongdoing."[31]

Though the Bible and salvation permeated all facets of community life, the children were not especially devoted to "things of the spirit." In school, children's meetings, "home-talks," and discipline, children absorbed much religious information, but like children of the outside world, carried little of it to the playground. The youthful games and adventures of Pierrepont Noyes were no different from those of boys on the outside. They were "Biblically educated, but not morally precocious."[32]

There is no evidence to suggest that children fared poorly in the Oneida system. They were well educated, and the community was generally commended by outsiders for the health and politeness of its youngsters. Complex marriage did place community children in a precarious position in their dealings with the community's hired hands and outside children. They were repeatedly reminded of, or taunted with, their "illegitimate" birth.

The new sacred history, the radical reorganization of the relation between religion and the world, and the freedom from legality that accompanied the new covenant not only required the creation of a vanguard community to realize the kingdom of heaven on earth, it also provided the warrant for a total restructuring of marital and familial institutions. Reform or renovation of existing arrangements could only maintain the world in its present religious condition. Once it was realized that the kingdom of heaven on earth was possible, it was the duty of the religiously inspired to take the necessary steps to bring it into being. The conventional marriage and family arrangement was not renounced as immoral or base, it was merely a vestige of an earlier religious era that required legality for religious discipline. Exclusive love and marriage were inappropriate for the new age of fulfillment and could be abandoned by the spiritually cleansed for the heavenly standard of amative and familial organization. Complex marriage was never considered an "experiment," it was the model of the heavenly order. Once the outside world had been regenerated and the virtues of complex marriage appreciated, it too would embrace the order of the kingdom of heaven on earth.

The future of the community and the kingdom of heaven on earth, the Bible communists realized, rested with the generations that would follow. "Genetic engineering" through stirpiculture would provide the fine silks for a new humanity, and heavenly institutions would provide the patterns and tailoring for a spiritually perfect youth.

Economic Life at the Oneida Community

Religion and economy, we have seen, clash on several fronts. First, economic activity may compete with religion for the individual's time, attention, and energy. Second, the self-interest, individualism, and economic calculation required in rational capitalism run counter to any religious ethic of brotherliness and communalism. And third, nineteenth-century economic growth brought both vast material fruits and the inhumanities and immoralities of early industrialization. Moral radicalism and economic conservatism enabled nineteenth-century religious leaders to straddle these issues. John Humphrey Noyes and the Oneida Community used their new sacred history and postmillennial theory of progress to transcend these tensions.

The Oneida communists adopted a system of communal property to eliminate material self-seeking and to realize the social and economic relations of the primitive Church. Communism was to be the quantum leap beyond worldly economic activity (which violated the spirit of Christ and Paul) to the imminent order of heaven on earth. Once granted admission, the assets of new members were managed collectively. Originally no written statement was rendered, but by 1864 legal suits from seceders for back wages were proving troublesome, so the community instituted a "contract" in which members accepted support and sustenance in lieu of wages. The community pledged, on the grounds of morality, to refund the property or its value should the member withdraw. The pledge was expressly declared not to be a legal obligation and members relinquished the right to demand payment, or to enforce the pledge by legal action. Refunds were left to the community's discretion and could be discontinued or revised at any time. In practice, seceders were refunded all property brought in or its equivalent. Those who had no property when they joined were sent on their way with clothing and $100. At the suggestion of James Towner, a lawyer who had joined the community, legal title was later vested in a committee of four in order to prevent any property claims from forcing dissolution of the association by the courts. The vesting of property in individuals brought no change in management or administration: it was merely a formal device to protect the community from outsiders.[33]

At its inception Noyes expected the community to be strictly agricultural and self-sufficient. Not only were his followers strongly committed, they were farmers and craftsmen who brought skills as well as savings to Oneida. The property registry, listing the value of property brought to the community from its commencement in 1848 until 1857, totaled $107,706.45. The first inventory, taken in 1857, showed only $41,740.00 remaining. Farming and publishing, the primary economic activity of the early community, lent insufficient support for the physical well-being of the Bible communists, and their diet and shelter were severely wanting. The publication of truth was considered "the art which stands nearest related to mind and spirit, and must take precedence over all other trades."[34] Throughout the community's history, its newspapers were available to all who were interested. Those who could afford to pay the nominal subscription fee—the estimated cost of production—were asked to do so; those who could not afford the price would be sent the newspaper free of charge; and those who could afford more than the stated cost were asked to pay enough to make up for the second group. The community newspaper consistently lost money. When Charles Nordoff visited Oneida in 1875, the *Oneida Circular* printed about 2,000 copies a week and lost $600 that year.[35] In earlier, leaner years publication costs were a substantial financial drain.

The community newspapers included articles and items on religion, reprints of Noyes's "home-talks" and essays, current events, community correspondence, a daily journal of community activities and events, articles on science written by members or reprinted from other publications, book reviews, articles of general interest, and advertisements for community business and publications. The wide breadth of the consecutively published *Circular* and the *Oneida Circular* never distracted from its primary concern—evangelism.

The economic shortcomings of farming and publishing were supplemented by commerce. The community raised, preserved, and sold fruits and vegetables, and it bought fine sewing silks, needles, and pins to be peddled throughout New England. These efforts failed to stop Oneida from losing money, and the property and savings of new members were counted on to slow the dwindling of capital. Economic solvency became possible with the help of Sewell Newhouse. Joining the community in 1848 from nearby Oneida Castle, Newhouse brought with him a secret process for animal-trap production. Newhouse did not part easily with his secret for turning springs. It took some time to coax the process out of him and make it a community asset. Trapmaking on a significant scale was begun in 1855. Newhouse traps were popular locally, and business flourished. By 1860 the Newhouse trap had become the standard in the United States and Canada, and for nearly seventy years all the steel traps used by the Hudson Bay Company were made at Oneida. Trap production soon became the main source of income and other industries sprang into being. Between 1857 and 1866 the community successfully manufactured and sold traveling bags and satchels, mop-holders, preserved fruits, and other small items. In 1866 Oneida began silkmaking, and tableware manufacture began at the Wallingford branch community in 1877.

After the sacrifices of early years, business brought a measure of luxury. In the early 1860s construction was begun on a brick Mansion House to replace the old wooden building constructed before the first winter. The task of rising above selfish interest meant there could be little in the way of personal indulgences; private living quarters and clothing were little more than functional. Jewelry and personal adornment were restrained but not forbidden, and criticism quickly brought excesses into line. Communal luxuries were another matter and could be unselfishly enjoyed by all. Mansion House public rooms were far more elaborate than the private and semiprivate living quarters, and with growing prosperity the community acquired a Turkish bath, a photographic studio, a chemical laboratory, musical instruments and props for theatrical productions, and a summer cottage on Oneida Lake.

Business success depended on God's grace, but never relied on Providence. New industries and changes in production, distribution, and sales were meticulously studied, taking potential risks and profits into account. Good business sense told the community that diversification would insulate it from fluctuations in individual markets. In 1863, the community even considered purchasing $10,000 of stock in the Bank of Indiana at Lafayette after a friendly believer, who happened to be a bookkeeper for this bank, said it was very profitable.[36]

The community observed that the world's repugnance to labor was because sheer necessity reduced labor to merely earning a living. Communism restored labor's spiritual and social virtues. The committee system, rotation of jobs, and the mingling of the sexes at work infused even the most menial and otherwise distasteful tasks with responsibility, enthusiasm, and vitality. Collective labor, attacking a distasteful or overwhelming task by a storm of many hands in what was called a "bee," created a convivial atmosphere that made work a joy. The various factories and workshops were equipped with the most modern machinery and labor-saving devices, some of which were the community's own invention. Training was available to both sexes for all occupations if one demonstrated interest and ability. Once the community attained a measure of economic prosperity the burden of labor was relatively light.[37]

For the first fifteen years member labor was sufficient to satisfy the demand for community products. The startling success of the Newhouse trap and the growing business acumen led Oneida to employ outside workers to fill the less desirable jobs. By 1871 the community employed about 150 outsiders. During peak business periods their numbers would swell to as many as 200.

The worldly wage system would not do for Oneida's outside help. Noyes considered the "hireling system" one small step above slavery and something that the community should take care not to be dragged down by. It was hoped that outside labor would only be temporary, but once it became apparent that the community depended upon supplementary workers, innovations to the wage system were introduced to add an element of civilization, refinement, and liberality. In 1871 the community had already erected comfortable housing for some of its hired workmen, and expected to make pleasant homes for many others. Working conditions in the factories, farms, and grounds were superior to those outside the community; free transportation was supplied to those who lived in neighboring towns, and Oneida became especially well known for its generous wages and amiable employee relations. Community concerts and entertainment were opened to employees and their families with the hope that the community would not contract the diseases of the world and outsiders would catch salvation.

Eventually the Oneida Community became a substantial industrial center. In 1864 the combined net worth of the Oneida and Wallingford communities was $185,000. By 1880 that figure had risen to $600,000.[38] Community industry, run as a rational profit-making concern, might be expected to create the same kinds of tensions between religion and world extant to outside utopian boundaries. Mere social reform or renovation of labor and property relations were insufficient for a community whose religious mission was its sole reason for being. Religious justifications were necessary for ideological support and completeness. For all its worldliness, business was to be subservient to religion as

a token of God's advancing conquest of the world. In the community business is kept pure and made acceptable to God . . . so far as business proceeds from a new center—the power driving the machinery is different from that of the world; as our points of contact increase, we shall expect to see one kind of business "log in" until the whole business world is won over to Christ.[39]

Business would be a tool of evangelism. The kingdom of heaven on earth would require an economic system as well as a political system to handle local needs. High ideals alone would not transform the world. The unregenerate would be "converted" by the undeniable success of the community's business and social program. Bible communism was the next step in the continuing progress of mankind and would have to be shown to be viable in Christian *and* economic terms. The age of fulfillment was one of progressive prosperity and happiness. As the vanguard of the kingdom of heaven on earth it was the obligation, if not the destiny, of the Oneida Community to move in that direction.

This is not to say that the community saw business as no threat to its religious ideals. The temptations to materialism, selfishness, and greed were carefully guarded against in "home-talks," criticism, and evening meetings. The ultimate priority of religion over business could never be questioned, but, on occasion, the issue could be circumvented if the community could arrive at an acceptable justification. In 1864, business demanded higher production than could be accomplished within the community's resources. The production crisis led to a debate on how to mobilize a larger work force without reaching outside the community. The members decided to forgo time devoted to study and self-improvement to meet the temporary demand for greater productivity, rather than hire outsiders or accept fewer orders. An elaborate casuistry was not needed to resolve this potential conflict of conscience. Poor calculation and overzealous sales, not a failure of theology or organization, had created a temporary production crisis, but the community's business principles and reputation—essential, as we have seen, to Bible communism's evangelism—were at stake. Increased community production at the expense of individual perfection was justified by Perfectionist merit in personal sacrifice for the sake of the community. Perfectability had to be both individual and collective; to deny one's communal obligations smacked of selfishness and self-seeking. The question of business needs over religious ideals was thus neatly avoided by keeping the community's economic activity within the context of a religious mission.[40]

Science and Education at the Oneida Community

Considering the rational support that science gave religion at the beginning of the nineteenth century, it should be no surprise that John Humphrey Noyes found science to be supportive of religiosity, by providing more profound knowledge of God's work, and by serving as an adjunct to revelation and inspiration. Science was one of the important progressive forces in the world—it was "catalytic, destructive, revolutionary," and at one with the spirit of Christ.[41]

In ideological terms science could be counted upon to reveal the rational grounds for faith and to provide a more intimate understanding of God's creation. In programmatic terms science advanced both individual and collective perfection. Perfect faith alone was insufficient for spiritual perfection. The mystical opening of the heart to the purifying power of the Holy Spirit had to coincide with an individual asceticism that sought to develop character and intellect. Science, with its discipline and contemplative rigors, was the strop on which reason's fine edge would be sharpened. The fruit of scientific thought, technology, was counted on to relieve humankind of its material trials, release it for more spiritual pursuits, and occasion the perfection of the physical world.

Science also offered the possibility of effecting humanity's biological perfection through selective breeding. On considering his wife's own trials and hardships in childbirth and its burden on womanhood in general, Noyes came to the realization that it is often poor policy to let "nature" take its course. His study of Malthus further reinforced his conviction that an effective system of birth control was an absolute necessity and gave his system of male continence a scientific foundation. But continence was more than a system of birth control, it also opened the way for scientific propagation. In the 1860s Noyes studied the work of Charles Darwin and Francis Galton (who coined the term "eugenics" in 1883), and considered the problem of scientific breeding. Darwin's discovery of natural selection led directly to voluntary selection for the improvement of mankind. If scientific selective breeding could vastly improve livestock, the same principles should be applied to human propagation. Stirpiculture provided the opportunity for man to use God's gift of reason and science to breed a physically, morally, and intellectually superior humanity. This step beyond nature was not an appropriation of God's power or the arrogance of mortals playing God—it was a fulfillment of God's will. Only the conventions of the world restrain us—the law of God commands us to move on. Noyes suggested that the community either make its convictions stronger and break society's restraints, or abandon its convictions altogether.[42]

The community shared Noyes's interest in science, and its newspapers contained original articles on science and technology, and reprinted articles from other sources covering the complete range of contemporary science. The *Circular*'s column, "Daily Journal," which recorded daily events and affairs, indicates that the community regularly held scientific discussions and invited professionals to speak on their work. The community was not content with mere discussion. A community journal entry in 1863 speaks of correspondence which the community opened with the Smithsonian Institution suggesting that a meteorological observation post be established at Oneida.[43]

Naturally, religious training was at the core of the community's educational program. Bible study and discussion of Perfectionist principles and practice went well beyond the community schoolrooms. The evening meeting was the primary arena for religious discussion, but any significant event—be it in the factory, fields, or playground—could provide an occasion and topic for religious education.

Secular education was hardly slighted, for the spiritual perfection sought by the Oneida communists was not limited to matters of religiosity, purity of heart, and sinless behavior. Progressive improvement required full development of all the powers and faculties of mind and body, and perfection meant the realization of the individual's full human potential. Children were schooled by the community and, when they were of age, could be sent to Harvard or Yale—though Yale was preferred—for higher education, training in law, medicine, engineering, or some other special skill needed by the community. In the fall of 1869 the Oneida Community established an "Embryo College" whose purpose was to give the rising generation a college education at home. Mathematics was given prominence in the educational program as the foundation of all the sciences. Study began with algebra, geometry, and trigonometry, and progressed to chemistry and physics. It was admitted that the community's education might take longer to complete than Yale's or Harvard's, but much was to be gained in keeping the young at home where their spiritual development could also be guided.

Education was by no means limited to the young. Courses in history, philosophy, Latin, French, and German, and mathematics and science were popular with adults.

Ultimately the Oneida Community paid a high price for sending its brightest and most talented into the world for higher education. By the 1870s science had achieved significant institutional and intellectual autonomy from religion, and the principled incompatibility of science and faith had made strong inroads in scientific and academic circles. The Oneida communists could successfully insulate themselves from these changes by using the same logic and rationale that had worked in the past: by attributing the conflict between science and religion to a misguided conception of the purpose of science, and by absorbing science into an overarching millennial scheme. When the community's best and brightest youth returned from Yale, they brought with them a strong taste for positive science and German rationalism, and a principled religious skepticism. Two "sciences" having different intellectual foundations now faced each other within the community and, as we shall see in the next chapter, the conflict that emerged threatened the Oneida Community's existence.

The Oneida Community seemed to have a sturdy theological foundation that resolved the tensions between religion and world, but the institutional vaults that gave form and structure to the utopian edifice proved, over time, to be vulnerable to stress. Democratic theocracy was merely superficially democratic, and viable only as long as religious consensus was maintained and the political elements of complex marriage remained below the surface. Complex marriage itself proved to be equally fragile, for its expressed purpose—universal love—was violated by ascending fellowship, its administrative form. A further, significant challenge to their amative arrangement came from a crusading clergy incensed at the community's theological and social-sexual innovations.

Economic prosperity, so important to the community's religious mission, would also become a locus for theological and political conflict, for it required rational planning and managerial and administrative efficiency. Theological consistency would require that economic criteria take a back seat to religion or that a strained casuistry account for departure from religious principles. These problems, we will see, were latent in the community's theology and emerged after communal material comfort and business success were realized and no longer only a hope for the future.

An ingenious reinterpretation of Christian history had resolved the tension between religion and world and united the two theoretically. Once that theology unfolded in practice, once it was made the basis for community building and action, there was a reemergence of tension between religion and world, between the Oneida Community and external society, and within the confines of utopia.

8
The Breakup of the
Oneida Community:
Reemerging Tensions
between Religion
and World

We have looked at religious utopia as a transcendental endeavor; as an attempt to go beyond the tension between religious ideals and worldly activity; as a communal effort forging valuative and normative consistency between religion and worldly pursuits. Utopian experiments seek a unified life in which religious ideals permeate all its aspects, so that life in the world itself becomes a religious experience. Religious utopias attempt to resolve the inherent contradiction between sacred and profane by creating a heavenly kingdom on earth.

We will examine the failure of the Oneida Community in terms of the failure of religious utopianism itself. Chapter 7 demonstrated how the Oneida Community used a new sacred history to transcend the tension between religion and world, and Oneida did succeed in transcending many of those tensions in nineteenth-century America, but new tensions surfaced that defied resolution. Although religion and world could be theoretically unified within the confines of the community, the external world remained an obdurate reality, a source of periodic antagonism and harassment. The borders of the Oneida Community became the locus of new tensions between religion and world. Changes in scientific theory, practice, and institutions and a policy of sending community youths to universities for specialized training made it impossible to insulate the Bible communists from a rising current of thought that found faith and science incompatible. The religious skepticism that accompanied current scientific thought undermined the religious consensus and legitimation that was crucial to democratic theocracy. Perfectionist doctrine and the success of the Newhouse trap propelled the community well beyond the subsistence economy characteristic of many utopian experiments. As a dynamic concern the community business required rational calculation, skilled management, and occupational specialization unfettered by religious principles, independent of the Perfectionist tenets that provided its justification. The departure from worldly exclusive love and adoption of complex marriage regulated by ascending fellowship led to new conflicts, not directly over the love objects, but over administration and the sexual perquisites of spiritual seniority. These tensions of the second order proved fatal. Utopian optimism gave way to skepticism and religious doubt. This seamless theological fabric became frayed and unraveled because its first thread, religious utopianism, could not be kept knotted.

The Interface of Utopia and "Extopia"

Utopian sects hold a dual, contradictory commitment to both evangelism and withdrawal. The world is the proper sphere of utopian activity and must be made consistent with an ideal image, yet it must also be held at a distance safe enough to prevent contamination. The utopian response to the world is thus fraught with ambivalence. As a consequence of this ambiguity sect leaders are often endowed with a considerable flexibility in policy, a factor contributing to the durability of religious utopian experiments. On the other hand, the components of utopianism—withdrawal and evangelism—are a continuous source of friction and generate many of the sect's serious internal conflicts.[1]

The Oneida communists demonstrated the contempt, aversion, and moral superiority characteristic of any group of believers who are firm in their conviction of being in the "true path" or of possessing "true knowledge." They were all originally of the world, but now they had risen above it, serving God's kingdom on earth. Worldly society and culture, and its religious, political, economic, intellectual, and sexual life, were grounded in an unregenerate, anachronistic spiritual and secular order serving values and authority well short of perfection and God. "True religion" and the "supreme government of God" were the Oneida Community's guiding principles and polity. The members paid taxes only because they were required to by law and it was necessary to court the good will of their neighbors. They neither voted nor participated in politics at any level. Noyes made his own declaration of independence from the government of the United States in 1837 and recalled those sentiments in the Putney Community's voice in 1843: "We are resident foreigners; citizens not of the United States, but of the Kingdom of Christ; and as such we claim the protection of the government of the United States, while we disclaim allegiance to it and participation in its evil deeds."[2]

Formation of a closed, select community of utopianists allows for new, and sometimes systematic, relationships between utopia and "extopia," the external social and cultural arena beyond utopian boundaries. For the Bible communists at Oneida the interface between utopia and extopia provided new opportunities for tension between religion and world.

Neighbors and townspeople found community members to be fair, honest, polite, and hardworking, and the community did its best to cultivate these qualities in its relationships with outsiders. Friendship with outsiders was another matter. The outside world not only tempted, it contaminated. The unregenerate world had not forsaken sin and the regenerate should fear the downward pull of these descending fellowships. Despite its spiritual aversion to outsiders, the community knew that its unorthodox family system depended upon the good will of its neighbors for survival. The community generously entertained thousands of guests yearly and its large lawn was a favorite picnic spot for visitors. After a day of tours and entertainment the building and grounds were scoured to remove any vestige of outsiders. Those who had regular contact with nonmembers were subjected to a similar "scouring" in mutual criticism.

The requisites of business success proved to be a continuous irritant to Perfectionist sensibilities for the same reason: community salesmen and business agents were particularly vulnerable to spiritual degradation because they traveled often and interacted with worldly businessmen. On returning from a business trip they underwent a spiritual and physical cleansing that included both mutual criticism and a Turkish bath.

The hireling system brought the outside world to community grounds and was a cause for concern from the beginning. In October 1877, Theodore Noyes, the chosen leader of the administrative council that then governed, stated his nervousness over contact with the "world." The contact that children had with outsiders was especially dangerous, and some of the boys were getting too well acquainted with the hired diningroom maids. This only further aggravated their irreverence. They had no earnest spirit of self-improvement, nor a keen ambition for education, and, of late, a number of young people had begun to hold attendance at the evening meetings lightly. Adults had not been immune from the "world" either, and many had become much too interested in attendance at the local Oneida Fair. Ann Hobart, then the "Leading Mother" of the community, further stated that members would be much happier if they cared less for the ways and fashions of the world, and the community would be better off when it had grown old enough so that all the members' relatives were inside.[3]

Conscription for the Civil War could have led to a serious confrontation with civil authority, but an oversight by the Madison and Oneida county enrolling officers—community members called it Providence—resulted in the issue's never being raised. The Oneida Community grounds were on the border of both counties. Each enrolling officer thought the community was in the other's jurisdiction. The local townspeople suspected foul play, but an investigation convinced them otherwise.

The community's objection to the war was not based on disbelief of the rightfulness of war, nor in the use of weapons—though it did consider war a poor way to defeat evil or settle differences. Its objection was based on the want of orders from the supreme government of God. The Civil War did tap the members' abolitionist sentiments and they followed the action closely, rejoicing with Union victories, agonizing over defeats. The community bore a full share of the financial burden of the war by lending money to the town of Oneida to help raise volunteers and commutation fees, and by aiding soldiers passing through.

As an alternative system of moral order, Oneida's theology was perceived as a threat by followers of more accepted religious convictions. The notoriety of complex marriage—associated with antinomian "free love" by many—and eugenics periodically aggravated the moral sensibility of local townspeople and clergy. During the 1860s and 1870s isolated sermons and articles coalesced into concerted opposition. The organized crusade by the clergy began in December 1878. A union of Presbyterians, Episcopalians, and Methodists was drawn together by Professor John W. Mears of Hamilton College—a perennial opponent of the Oneida Community—and meetings were held in Syracuse, New York. Mears and his clerical supporters condemned the wrongs done to society by the Oneida Community's flagrant violation of Christian morality and called for its suppression. When the Oneida Community abandoned complex marriage in August 1879, Mears and his colleagues were satisfied.

The outside opposition to complex marriage had been formidable. Mears and other self-styled guardians of American morals such as Arthur Comstock did their best to marshal public opinion against Oneida, but the community was confident it could withstand the attack.[4] Only when internal dissent over complex marriage grew and unity of purpose could not be counted on, did the community submit. It was not a question of renouncing the practice; Noyes and his circle still stood by its purpose. Internal weakness made the community more vulnerable to outside attack, and complex marriage was abandoned in order to save the community as a whole. As we will see in greater detail, the interface between utopia and extopia proved threatening to the community's existence only after internal conflicts defied control. Oneida could no longer draw moral strength from rejection by the world and lapsed into "apathetic introversionism." Relinquishing all hope of transforming the world, regarding it with suspicion and hostility, the community became preoccupied with the practical concerns of its life.[5]

Administration of the Government of God

The fading charisma of John Humphrey Noyes has been a feature in many explanations of the community's failure. It was a combination of Noyes's personal charisma and his radical theology that made the synthesis of religion and world at Oneida possible, but the decline of charismatic authority started long before the breakup of the community. Noyes advanced the rationalization of his theology by taking every opportunity to systematize his thought. *The Berean* (1847), a collection of his writings, became the community bible. Recognizing the community's need to support itself economically and the prophetic need for structural permanence, Noyes directed the routinization of his charisma from the beginning by creating a complex institutional structure to oversee Oneida's many activities.

Stable institutional structures, anathema to personal charisma in Weber's terms, were well in place at Oneida in the 1850s, but Noyes was still able to exert considerable power by virtue of his personal talents and spiritual virtuosity. He never dictated policy in a naked, authoritarian fashion, but he was able to easily forge consensus to his

views. He retained, until his later years, what Joseph Bensman and
Michael Givant have called "pseudo-charisma": "the means, imag-
ery, the appearance of charismatic leadership as a rational device by
which rationally calculating leadership groups attempt to achieve or
maintain power."[6]

In the 1860s and 1870s age prematurely took its toll on John
Humphrey Noyes. His always feeble voice faded to a whisper,
and his hearing so degenerated he was left out of the reach of ordinary conversation. In these years, Noyes spent much of his time
away from Oneida, leaving the day-to-day affairs to his trusted
lieutenants. During the period of waning involvement in the community, Noyes made his worst mistake; he declared his first son,
Dr. Theodore Noyes, to be his heir to leadership.

Theodore Noyes, intelligent, trained in medicine, and a proven effective manager of the community businesses, had been leaving and
returning to the community periodically as he wrestled with religion
and his father's displeasure. By 1875 he was fully reconciled with his
father and at least partially reconciled with his father's religion.
Theodore was rather open about his spiritual vacillation and unen-
thusiastically acquiesced to his father's nomination. The community
was open and vehement in its opposition. As intelligent and efficient
as he was, the community found him far too wanting in religion and
spirituality. John Humphrey Noyes withdrew his nomination. Not
until 1877, after several rejections, did the community accept
Theodore as John Humphrey Noyes's successor, and the elder Noyes
retired to devote his time to writing and study.

Theodore's tenure lasted only until 1878. The community felt he
was straying from its ideals and had openly discussed his religious
skepticism. John Humphrey Noyes returned to Oneida, and after a
head-on collision with his father, Theodore resigned and the elder
Noyes resumed leadership. In the form of a will, John Humphrey
Noyes stated that if he should die before Theodore was restored in
the community's faith and leadership, a committee of thirty-five
named persons should take charge and make provisions for government that seemed wisest.

This is a brief account of a very turbulent period in the community's history, but it highlights the incongruity of democratic theocracy. Theodore was not the only unbeliever among the younger generation. Many shared Theodore's religious skepticism, some embraced science and agnosticism as an alternative to Perfectionism.
Democratic theocracy could only work under a charismatic or

"pseudo-charismatic" leader who could count on the community's consensus on religion and the leader's role as divine representative. Once the religious base of the community had been fractured, the "old school" Oneida Perfectionists saw the community's purpose threatened, and it opposed John Humphrey Noyes and encouraged a community revivalism more to the members' liking. By the same token, religious skeptics and unbelievers did not see John Humphrey Noyes as an inspired link with God, Jesus, and Paul. He became merely an aging autocrat, a vestige of an earlier religious era. Factionalism over religion and complex marriage elevated democracy over inspiration, and John Humphrey Noyes eventually handed community leadership over to an administrative council that Myron Kinsley, as his agent, nominated and submitted to the community for changes and approval.

With the crisis of leadership and succession engendered by Theodore Noyes's turbulent tenure and his father's moving in and out of command, nagging doubts about the community's survival lent an undercurrent of anxiety to the perennial utopian optimism. The values, norms, customs, and conventions of the outside world loomed large. Breaking with these codes had its own set of problems, but commitment, community, charismatic leadership, an absolute set of values, and the excitement of embarking on a social and religious experiment provided promise, support, and sustenance. Returning from utopia threatened alienation, intolerance, and an individualism that older members had not known for thirty years and youth had not experienced at all.

The Emerging Conflict between Science and Religion

Science presented no problem to the Oneida Community in its early years because science was then perceived either as a handmaiden to religion confirming revelation and Scripture, or as God's gift as a means of better understanding his creation. The conflict between science and religion at Oneida did not emerge over a specific point of theology or scientific understanding, but over the awareness by scientifically educated youth that these spheres of knowledge were incommensurable. Religion and positive knowledge, they had discovered at Yale, were based on radically different epistemological and ontological premises. Young community members studying science, medicine, and philosophy returned home with more than specialized knowledge; they brought skepticism, doubt, and absolute rational criteria for knowledge and facts. When Oneida Perfectionism confronted scientific skepticism it could neither defend itself on scientific grounds nor convince the young intellectuals of the unity of inspiration and science. Although some were able to accommodate or reconcile these contradictory perspectives, or at least keep the problem to themselves, others could not or would not. Whether this new conception of a science that was opposed to faith generated open or quiet religious skepticism, it fractured the spiritual unity that had been the source of the community's strength nonetheless.

In 1870, the same year Noyes announced the success of sending young men to Yale for scientific and technical education, the community began to complain privately and in their evening meetings that the scientific training and concerns of the young people had put a damper on the religious aspects of the evening meeting. In response to family fears, Noyes reaffirmed the unity of science and inspiration:

I should advice [sic], therefore, that the spiritually minded look favorably toward science, and that the scientifics look favorably toward faith, and see if God will not bring the hearts of these long separated classes together. Then I think we shall have lively meetings. I am not sure but there is more real Divine inspiration going on in the scientific world than in the religious world. Cant and legality and timidity are death to inspiration. If we want lively meetings, we want inspiration; and if we want inspiration, let us follow it where we find it. If it is among the scientifics let us honor it there, even if the scientifics themselves think it is only their own zeal and sagacity. For my part I consider the success of our young men in science as the effect of inspiration, and I claim their victories as the victories of faith. And we must train these young men to acknowledge that it is so. Then they will be the beginning of a new class of scientists, more humble and more successful than the world has ever seen; and then they will cast their crowns at the feet of faith, and turn their whole strength into our religious meetings.[7]

In part this was a generational problem and, unfortunately for the community, several promising young members did not take Noyes's advice to heart and began questioning bondage to the Bible and religion. Daniel Bailey was a brilliant young man who had been crippled by an accident early in life and became a leader among rising young community intellectuals. He was criticized for his religious skepticism and for holding too much "sympathy with German poetry, German thought in general, and positivism in particular." Another young intellectual, Joseph Skinner, was much under Bailey's influence, and shared his skepticism. On April 10, 1872, Skinner departed, no longer able to live in a religious community in good conscience.

In the mid-1860s, Theodore Noyes was in close sympathy with his father's religious beliefs. Along with Bailey and Skinner, Dr. Noyes became intrigued, then won, by German rationalism and positivism and lapsed into disbelief. He left the community on July 3, 1873, to seek his fortune on the outside. Soon after leaving he wrote his father asking to return. Theodore realized an arrangement would have to be made to effect his readmittance. He offered several options, including feigning belief, but preferred to return as a confirmed nonbeliever partaking fully in the nonreligious aspects of community life. It was Theodore's hope that Oneida would become a nonsectarian community that would leave religion to individual conscience. The elder Noyes rejected his son's preference, but invited him to return in the hope of his reconversion. Theodore did return on July 15 and agreed to try to believe as a conscious act rather than as an act of spontaneous faith. To return Theodore to the religious fold, John Noyes commissioned his son to conduct a scientific study of spiritualism, hoping it would restore his belief in the immortality of the soul. After a year of enthusiastic study and experiment Theodore reported his scientific evidence supporting spiritualism and announced he had made substantial progress in his own spiritual rehabilitation.

Theodore was on the road to reconciliation with his father, but after 1870 a significant segment of the most talented young adults—those whom the family counted on for future leadership—were religious skeptics, agnostics, or quiet atheists. Although confirmed unbelievers were nowhere near the majority, their intellectual prominence and influence on the young convinced older members that the second generation was slipping into disbelief.

Spiritual disunity and intellectual conflict struck at the taproot of community strength. Without the support of unanimous religious conviction, the perception of a religious mission—the community's historical reason for being—eroded. The family could not be confident that external pressure would be met with a united community voice, or that the future was in any way secure. The spiritual division that arose from the conflict between science and religion in the early 1870s would cast a long shadow on community events, culminating in the abandonment of utopia in 1881.

Abandoning Complex Marriage

For thirty years, complex marriage had been the institutional core of the community. It successfully stemmed the exclusiveness, selfishness, and propertylike relations between the sexes and enabled Perfectionists to carry out universal love and brotherhood preached by Jesus, Paul, and the primitive Church. It seemed as if the tension between religion and world in regard to love, sex, and family had been transcended.

By 1879, growing dissatisfaction over the administration of complex marriage led to extensive debate, and factions crystallized around the issue of initiation of virgins into the sexual life of the community. The initiation of young men never posed a problem: they routinely entered the sexual community at puberty. The difficulty arose with young women. John Humphrey Noyes, with the common consent of the community, always introduced them to sex when they came of age. When he grew older, he sometimes delegated the role of "first husband" to the central members. William A. Hinds, a member since Oneida's founding, and James W. Towner, a recent but highly regarded member, questioned Noyes's right to decide. When the opposition went public, approximately thirty members joined to form a highly agressive party protesting Noyes's authority. The "Townerites," as the opposition was called, complained of Noyes's autocratic government, called for a freer system of complex marriage without the restraints of ascending fellowship, and wanted a greater voice in the management of community business. The "Noyesites" stuck by Noyes and the present system. These factions cut across all apparent divisions within the community—across old and young, central and peripheral, and religious and nonreligious members.

Possessiveness and jealousy had supposedly been eliminated in the love relationship, but had sprung up anew over the "privileges" that went with a high level of spirituality. According to the precepts of complex marriage, all community members were "married" to all others and no individual could assume or lay claim to an exclusive bond or affection for another. Theoretically, acceptance of such a system, coupled with support and sanction in mutual criticism, would reduce jealousy to an aberration indicative of alienation, nonconformity, inharmonious behavior, lack of dedication to community principles, or a faulty integration into the emotional and sexual life of the community. Jealousy was considered a social rather a natural reaction innate to humans.

John Humphrey Noyes, as we have seen, was well aware of the propertylike nature of exclusive love, marriage, and jealousy, and he created complex marriage to elevate love to a purely amative and spiritual level. Further elaboration of the love-property analogy will expose the inherent problem of complex marriage and the particular conflicts the arrangement generated.

Although love is not strictly a property relationship, it may develop propertylike features. In its first phase, "rivalry," competitors vie for the attention and affections of the love object. The second phase, "securing of position," establishes the successful competitor's claim. In the third phase, "trespass," this claim may be defied or the new rival may be ignorant of its existence. The fourth stage, "resolution," reestablishes or breaks the propertylike claim, which may result in a new round of rivalry. Jealousy may come into play only in the second, third, or fourth phases, for in the rivalry phase a propertylike claim has yet to be recognized, though it is anticipated.[8]

If exclusive love were abandoned, jealousy would become an unacceptable display of un-Christian emotion. Giving up the propertylike aspect of love, sex, and family meant giving up the security of an emotional claim. All that remained was rivalry without resolution and unrelenting sexual tension and competition. The privileges and perquisites of ascending fellowship mitigated that tension to some degree, but because the love objects themselves could not be openly coveted it became the locus for sublimated sexual and romantic jealousy.

The propertylike nature of love relationships allows for the norms and sanctions that govern illegitimate rivalry and trespass to be negotiated, which reaffirms and reinforces the property relationship and establishes limits to competition. Once a claim is successfully made—recognized as legitimate by the claimee, the love object, and the wider community of significant others—"illegitimate" competitors and trespassers are expected to withdraw gracefully or suffer community sanctions. Jealousy on the part of the legitimate owner is justifiable if not mandatory, and envy on the part of illicit rivals is unacceptable. Nonexclusive love and the sanctions of mutual criticism made jealousy, envy, and a graceful withdrawal unacceptable, because all are based on selfishness and the exclusiveness of property. Sexual and romantic rivalry could not be "settled" and could escalate into a more fundamental conflict. What began as individual envy of the sexual privileges of high religious status could only be ex-

pressed at a different level, as a criticism of complex marriage,
ascending fellowship, and the community as a whole. Sublimated
rivalry for love objects found its highest expression in rivalry for
power and criticism of Noyesian "despotism."

For a community so used to harmony and consensus, the factionalism that grew out of the administration of complex marriage only
fueled the anxiety already present from the crisis of leadership and
succession. Because the community's viability and future were in
doubt, much community thought turned to the consequences of
complex marriage should the community dissolve and its members
be thrust into the world. In his journal entry for February 2, 1879,
Francis Wayland-Smith—a young, independent-thinking intellectual who along with Theodore Noyes and Edwin Burnham headed
the "Third Party" opposing the Townerites—wrote of the growing
undercurrent of dissatisfaction with the nature of sexual fellowship:

The young people as a class, and some of the older ones, are free to speak of
their preference for a more limited sexual fellowship than Mr. Noyes has always advocated. The more bold and ultra of them cooly declare in favor of a
monogamic relation. . . . [This ought not be called] *public* sentiment for it is
by no means expressed publicly. I mean that it is a spreading feeling, already
embracing quite a class. Mr. Noyes feels himself so strong that he does not
meddle with it, even if he is fully aware of it. [It is a dangerous state of things
in that] it is one which cannot but be destructive to the present organization
of the Community, if it continues unopposed.[9]

By June 1879, Professor Mears had organized considerable religious criticism against the community's sexual practices. Clerical opposition to Oneida Perfectionism had not brought down the community in the past, so Mears was marshaling political and legal forces to
dismantle what he considered a crime worse than Mormon polygamy. On Saturday, June 21, 1879, John Humphrey Noyes read of his
imminent arrest and trial for the community's sexual practices in a
Syracuse newspaper. The next evening he secretly fled to Canada
without delegating authority to anyone. A considerable number of
members had been quietly calling for his departure or deposition
anyway, but the community was now left leaderless and the outside
threat that drove Noyes away remained. From Niagara Falls, Noyes
and Myron Kinsley, his trusted lieutenant, nominated nineteen
members to an administrative council. Kinsley was directed by
Noyes to take whatever steps he felt necessary without fear of losing

his support. Kinsley secured community support for the council, and it was empowered to conduct social and domestic affairs for the family.

The question of complex marriage was first raised in the administrative council early in August 1879. It began with a recommendation by William Hinds—who, besides being a member since Oneida's founding, was also a council member and a Townerite of late—that stirpiculture be suspended in the face of outside attacks and the tenuousness of community solidarity. Francis Wayland-Smith presented, and Dr. Theodore Noyes supported, an amendment to Hinds's resolution, proposing sexual intercourse be suspended altogether until the community was convinced its spiritual direction and mission had been reestablished, leadership renewed, control of errant youth recovered, and that it had once again "risen to a higher plane of morality than that of the world and were living under a higher government."[10] In the Wayland-Smith–Noyes amendment, complex marriage was inextricably linked to religion, John Humphrey Noyes's inspiration, and community control. In the chess game of community politics, Hinds, Towner, and Burnham—the core Townerites—had their principal pieces pinned by the Wayland-Smith–Dr. Noyes maneuver. If they voted against the amendment it would be seen as an open repudiation of John Humphrey Noyes. The Townerites' rejection of the amendment would have also implied that complex marriage should be a *natural* right equivalent to the free-love platform repudiated by the community. If they voted for the amendment, they would put themselves in a bad light with their own followers and deprive the whole family of a high privilege.

The council hotly debated the resolution and its amendment but remained deadlocked. Harriet Noyes Skinner, John Humphrey's sister, wrote to Noyes on the council's behalf for his advice. His reply came on August 20, 1879. The advice he had to offer, explained Noyes, did not result from weighing the arguments of the parties involved and taking sides. His recommendation came as inspiration to him. His utmost hope was for the community to hold together despite factionalism and disagreement over its social relations. Living in the outside world, he could clearly see that even given the community's present problems, it was still head and shoulders above the world. The proposal he was about to advance would keep the two fundamental motives of the community alive: the religious motive that looked toward heaven, and the worldly "bread-and-butter" motive of the business organization that sheltered and fed with "unfailing momentum." Complex marriage should be abandoned, not for Shakerism or worldly marriage but for "Paul's plan," which Noyes claimed recognized marriage but preferred singleness and celibacy.

The community should continue to hold and preach its social theory, "not conceding any consciousness of wrong in our practice, but conforming to worldly custom for the sake of avoiding offense, and we must still hold Complex Marriage as the true, rational, and final status which we look forward to as loyally as ever." Communism of persons was to be abandoned, communism of property, business, and household maintained. Male continence and regulated propagation should continue under community control enforced by mutual criticism. This new departure would induce the clergy to leave the community alone and encourage its new direction. Complex marriage had become divisive; Paul's plan allowed for choice between marriage and celibacy, encouraging harmony and respect for individual preference.[11]

Loyalists strongly supported the new departure. Hinds and Burnham were reluctant, fearing worldly marriage was a perilous undertaking that would endanger the most important principles of community life; they privately preferred a more liberal free-love arrangement. The family voted unanimously for John H. Noyes's "inspiration," with William Hinds abstaining. On August 28, 1879, at 10 A.M., complex marriage ended. Not all were enthusiastic, for many besides Hinds feared marriage would undermine the Oneida system. To outsiders the new departure was presented as a Christian surrender to public sensibilities with no mention of the internal debate or fragility of community harmony. The press gave the move glowing reviews, and Professor Mears promised support if the step was taken in earnest.

Noyes expressly preferred celibacy over marriage, but many community members rushed to nuptials nonetheless. Just like ordinary outsiders, the Bible communists vied for each other's attentions, and romantic rivalry and gossip surged through the community. Though no petition was expected to be denied, the council required an application and waiting period before the marriage ceremony would be performed. Even this mere formality was too much for some, and the community suffered an elopement soon after complex marriage ended. The offending couple subsequently apologized and was readmitted.

Although complex marriage was abandoned, Noyes felt stirpiculture could continue within the new familial system—"circumscribed marriage." Monogamous, legal marriage now became the best means available for advancing stirpiculture. Foremost, the community enclosure was to remain intact by keeping marriage within the community. The first step in stirpiculture had been to breed from the best, and the first generation of "stirps" had lived up to expectations. The next step was to "breed in and in," and here monogamous marriage provided no obstacle. Noyes proposed that married couples have all the children they wish within circumscribed marriage.[12] The paper was read to the Oneida Community, and serious opposition to free propagation rose as many questioned the advisability of bringing more children into an already threatened community. Circumscribed marriage and its stirpicultural aims were quietly dropped.

The first renewed tension between religion and world was supplied by the community's moral and religious opponents. Though external pressure was significant, it had been defeated in the past and showed signs that it could be beaten back again. Mears was terribly persistent. Friendly local political officials assured Oneida that Mears had no legal grounds on which to threaten the community, but their assurance was to no avail. Mears sought disaffected ex-members who would testify to knowledge of statutory rape or the corruption of morals of minors. Mears accumulated a vast amount of literature on the community's sexual practices and hoped to prosecute Oneida under the provisions of the Comstock Anti-Obscenity Law, but the community had stopped its open distribution of literature on complex marriage and male continence when the law was passed and were considered safe on that count. Friendly outsiders and knowledgeable community members felt the worst Mears could do was to launch an extended program of moral intimidation. The Oneida Community could count on strong local support and probably could have waited out the storm had its internal unity and resolve not deteriorated.

Complex marriage generated its own tensions over ascending fellowship. Finding love and emotional fulfillment circumscribed by ascending fellowship left smoldering embers of resentment. Youth found that spiritual and romantic love might not intersect, and, when it did, it could be separated by the community if proper restraint was not shown. Community love often became an intricate affair of private intimacy and public distance seasoned with spiritual self-doubt, public castigation or confession, separation, and romantic alienation. Jealousy over the sexual privileges of those high on the ladder of ascending fellowship generated more serious internal conflict. Outright attack on complex marriage would not have met with general support, because it was the religious basis of the community. Sexual jealousy was sublimated into conflict over the administration of complex marriage, and escalated into the question of the continuing inspiration of John Humphrey Noyes and the debate over community leadership.

The first problem, exclusive love and romance, was far easier to handle because it could be dealt with on an individual basis. For the most part, but not exclusively, it was a problem with the youngest adults, and they could be criticized and then excused by their emotional and spiritual immaturity. The second problem was much more intractable, for it was raised by mature adult members to whom the community would soon turn for leadership. This problem could not be individualized, because it was no longer a question of exclusive relationships; it became a challenge to Noyes's inspiration and leadership. The Townerites had a considerable constituency, albeit a minority, so their dissatisfaction with ascending fellowship could not be denounced as emotional selfishness or a naked play for individual power. The tension between religion and worldly jealousy re-emerged on a different level; not over the love object as property, for that was forbidden, but over the restraints and prerogatives of ascending fellowship.

With complex marriage no longer viable, Noyes offered anew Paul's plan to transcend the tension between religion and world. Celibacy—as the more spiritual option—did not generate a great amount of enthusiasm among the young. For the most part, the younger members did not share their elders' religious enthusiasm, and celibacy could only be justified in religious terms. Marriage offered relief from one of the younger members' serious complaints; it offered romantic love that did not have to meet the spiritual requirements of ascending fellowship and Perfectionism. In a community that elevated sexual pleasure to the status of sacrament in which partners communed with each other and with God, alternative means to religious ecstasy could be found, but meditation, Bible classes, and study did not hold much promise compared to sexual ecstasy as sacrament.

The abandonment of complex marriage was the first step in the dissolution of the utopian community as a whole. Universal love and communism of property were made possible by the elimination of the exclusive nuclear family. In allowing the nuclear family Noyes believed all failed utopian experiments had erred. The family brought about selfish concern for one's own kin, the treatment of women and children as property, and selfishness over material goods and wealth. Paul's plan tried to maintain utopian transcendence in an impossible fashion. Worldly marriage was recognized, celibacy preferred, and the religious and spiritual legitimacy of complex marriage maintained only as an ideal for the future.

The unified utopian religious experience had broken down into separate spheres of religion and world. Worldly familial exclusivity and material acquisitiveness returned with worldly marriage even though it was negatively sanctioned. Because the individual now had an alternative source of emotional support and material interest, community sanctions such as mutual criticism became much less effective. One's well-being and self-perception no longer exclusively depended on the community. Monogamous marriage and the reformation of family within the community reduced the Oneida Community to an economic communism, one that could not withstand family haggling over power and material rewards.

Production, Administration, and Oneida's Economic Ideology

A. J. MacDonald had been a chronicler of American socialist experiments and a visitor and friend of the Oneida Community. After MacDonald's death, John Humphrey Noyes acquired his notes and incorporated them with his own research and ideas to form *History of American Socialisms*, which was published in 1870. Noyes gave much thought to the numerous Owenite and Fourierist experiments and concluded that their fondness for agriculture and large tracts of land had much to do with their failure. Farming was by far the longest, hardest, and most uncertain road to fortune, and conflicting theories and methods were sure to lead to discord. The need for large tracts of land led socialists either to the wilderness or to out-of-the-way places far from railroads and markets. Socialist communities, if they were to leap ahead of civilization, had to limit their land investments to a minimum, stay near transportation and business centers, and put their energies into manufacturing as soon as possible. "Almost any kind of a factory would be better than a farm for a Community nursery."[13]

Self-sufficiency was only the first step for Oneida. The bounty of the kingdom of heaven on earth had to be more than merely adequate; it had to be abundant and prosperous to fulfill its religious promise and evangelical mission. The world must be offered incontrovertible proof that Bible communism provides both security of salvation and from material want, and assurance as well that religion and business need not clash. Though confident in his convictions, Noyes held no delusions that the temptations of lucre had been defeated once and for all, and he took every opportunity to remind the community that its was first and foremost a religious mission. Community newspapers, mutual criticism, and evening meetings provided forums for condemning selfishness, materialism, and worldliness in community business affairs.

The Oneida Community had been able to transcend the tension between religion and world through its radical reorganization of Christian theology and its progressive-millennialist scheme of history. Religious justifications could legitimate a growing, profit-making, economic organization, but a rational business structure required more than inspiration; it depended upon specialized skills, expert leadership, decision making based upon calculation, and the elimination of irrational interferences such as religion or ideology. These characteristics of rational economy were the locus of reemerging tension between religion and world in the community's economic sphere.

The community rotated its members' jobs for several reasons. First, in that way intellectual as well as manual skills were honed, allowing the individual to develop all facets of character to their fullest extent. Spiritual perfection required that all the coarse materials that God provided be polished to a saintly sheen. Second, job rotation was egalitarian, preventing invidious, unbrotherly distinctions arising from labor. Even the most talented had to be occasionally humbled by kitchen duty or field work for their own spiritual benefit. Third, variety made for enthusiasm. A change in routine, new tasks and co-workers, and temporary assignments created excitement and sociability. Dull or menial labor became tolerable, if not enjoyable.

Expansion of community manufacturing, diversification, and growing prosperity made job rotation inappropriate in many instances. Department heads, supervisors, and highly skilled and able members could not be rotated without seriously disrupting production. The continued patronage of Oneida's growing list of customers could not be tampered with by inefficiency and late deliveries. Rapidly expanding community business required planning and research for capital investment and improved productivity—skills not evenly distributed throughout the community. Growing manpower requirements necessitated hiring outsiders to do the least skilled, dull, and menial work in order to free members for more demanding tasks. As business prospered fewer and fewer members could be shifted, and the occupational structure of the community grew more rigid. Department heads and supervisors were now criticized for establishing their own occupational fiefdoms, garnering personal privilege, stature, and inflated egos from community work, and they were warned against creeping worldliness in their labor. As we have already noted, the hireling system created its own problems that required continuous religious and economic justification.

Eighteen sixty-seven was a troublesome business year for Oneida.[14] The annual report called the results satisfactory, but a serious "cash-flow" problem had made the year a difficult one. Oneida was free of debt at the beginning of the year, but by fall, when the various community businesses needed capital to prepare for incoming orders, liabilities exceeded cash assets by $59,000. Dr. Theodore Noyes was called in to direct community financial affairs and turn things around. Possessing exceptional leadership and managerial skills and great business acumen, Dr. Noyes, along with a new generation of young board members brought in on his coattails, were remarkably successful. By 1869 the community was free of debt, had $20,000 in surplus cash invested in U.S. bonds, and looked to Theodore for future leadership. With the easing of financial pressure, Dr. Noyes, as director of Community Industries, embarked on a new expansion program despite his father's cautious counsel of economy and restraint.

Young men occupied nearly all the important business positions, and there was much talk of "putting the older generation on the shelf" and running the community business as a strictly money-making venture. The business board no longer met in open session, having replaced public meetings with private conferences. Grumbling within the community came to a head in January 1872, when the whole business administration was brought up for discussion. John Humphrey Noyes spoke out for more spirituality in business, claiming his son did not appreciate the role of inspiration and relied too much on ability and financial machinery. Furthermore, the elder Noyes continued, business affairs should be open to the community for examination and alteration. The discussion that followed led to a reorganization of community business and Theodore Noyes's nervous breakdown and retirement to a sanatorium. He would not re-enter community business affairs for several years.

Not only was Theodore discredited, the incident began a debate that would continue for the duration of Oneida's utopian years, centering upon religious principles versus rational economic action. We must remember that the first cracks in religious consensus had already appeared, and Theodore's "fall from grace" was also a defeat for the rising generation. Having proven they could successfully govern the community's business affairs, they were censured for their accomplishment. Throughout the 1870s the business board was called to task for its lack of religion. In 1876 a converted Theodore Noyes reentered the fray on behalf of the spirit and announced that:

When those young men who have bright faculties drift away from spirituality, shirking the struggle we must undergo to purify our souls, and take refuge in the excitements of business, I think we are lucky to have some left of the sterner sort, who make a serious study of ethical and spiritual problems, and if I have any voice, they shall have a large place. The Community is ruined when it tucks its philosophers and spiritually minded off in a corner and gives its heart to money-making.

Theodore later resigned his business superintendency and retired to the Wallingford Community "to separate himself from the temptations of the world and seek a new spiritual experience."[15]

With the end of complex marriage, the already precarious, yet financially successful, economic communism was shaken further. Establishment of the nuclear family unit on a communitywide basis brought with it the very same economic individualism and family selfishness that the Bible communists had rejected in the world.

As 1880 approached, the community turned its attention to the appointment of a new administrative council for the coming year. The council, recognizing the community was divided into Loyalist and Townerite parties, feared that a vicious political battle over new appointments would bring the community to a sudden, shattering end. John H. Noyes was asked to make the appointments as he had for the first council. By then, a third party had emerged around Theodore Noyes, Francis Wayland-Smith, and Edwin S. Burnham. These three men each wrote to John H. Noyes claiming the administrative council had failed as a means of government. Rather than healing the rifts in the community, it had only widened them. The community could not return to the past, and the present arrangement would not hold much longer. The third party recommended a new departure: the formation of a joint-stock company in which members would be given shares and would vote for managers and directors. This modified communism, in the form of an economic co-operative, would defuse the powder keg of internal religious differences that threatened to destroy the community. This was not a breakup; it was planned to be a change in the distribution of profits and management that would keep the community together, maintain the business enterprises, and secure the future for its children and elderly. Moreover, individuals or groups could sell their shares and leave without forcing the community to dissolve.[16]

John Humphrey Noyes was surprised to hear of dissatisfaction with the administrative council, having been under the impression it had worked well. Myron Kinsley had his highest confidence and nominated the last council with his approval, Noyes reminded the council, and, if it was agreeable to the community, Kinsley would do so again. At an evening meeting the community accepted John H. Noyes's judgment and Myron Kinsley nominated the second administrative council. Blessed with Noyes's support and the general desire to avoid confrontations, the new council was accepted. As to the third party's recommendations, Noyes was noncommittal.

At the July 18, 1880, evening meeting, the council proposed a commission for reorganization to explore possible solutions to the community's internal problems. In August the commission reported to the community and recommended the Oneida Community divide and immediately reorganize as a joint-stock company. Members would be issued stock and given the opportunity to work for the company. The education of youth and support for the elderly would be assumed by the corporation. The details of the agreement to divide and reorganize were hammered out in September. On January 1, 1881, the Oneida Community became the Oneida Community, Ltd., and their religious utopian era came to a close.[17]

The joint-stock holders embraced individual money-making as enthusiastically as they had rejected it in the community's early years. Members had received a small cash allowance in the past for the purchase of personal incidentals outside the community, but since the community itself met all basic economic needs, money and the thought of personal wealth and property had never been taken too seriously, except as topics for criticism. After reorganization, as Pierrepont Noyes explains, money matters and property were approached with a seriousness taken to comical proportions:

During the first months of joint-stock our elders developed an exaggerated respect for private property, and an earnest search for opportunities to earn money. I remember an extraordinary business transaction in which Miss Jerusba Thomas exhibited this new passion of acquisitiveness in a way as unusual as her very unusual face. She insisted on measuring my hands, saying that she desired to knit me a pair of mittens. Then, after I had worn the mittens several days, she turned up with a bill for forty-five cents which my mother paid.[18]

Economic prosperity and industrial success were critical elements of the Oneida Community's theology and of their utopian and evangelical mission. With the unification of religious and economic principles and practice, the conflict between the two spheres that had been so troubling to John H. Noyes's contemporaries and predecessors had been resolved theologically. Community economic life yielded remarkable results, but the community's "calling" for prosperity required resort to rationalized economic principles and administration that overwhelmed the religious character of Bible communism. The economic ethos of Oneida Perfectionism thus contained its own contradiction: fulfillment of its economic mission split the ideological unity of religion and economy, and raised the same questions of religious and economic priorities that were being debated in the outside world.

This chapter has shown that the transcendence of the tensions between religion and the political, intellectual, sexual-familial, and economic spheres made possible by Noyes's brilliant reinterpretation of Christian history and Scripture was limited to the ideological level. First, the boundary between utopia and extopia became the frontline for conflicts with the outside world. Second, the government of God required administration and political order, and charismatic rulership and democratic theocracy ultimately proved to be insufficient to maintain the unity of religion and political order. With the decline of charismatic leadership and the fragmentation of religious consensus, democratic theocracy fell prey to factionalism, and democratic and theocratic sentiments clashed. Third, talented youth returning from Yale brought with them a new science and philosophy incompatible with religion. A sophisticated, independent scientific worldview introduced religious skepticism and shattered religious unanimity. Fourth, complex marriage and ascending fellowship generated intense conflicts over their administration, for the love objects themselves could not be openly coveted. Finally, economic success, central to the community's religious promise, created conflicts over business practices and their place within religious life. On all fronts, the tension between religion and world had been re-established and defied further resolution.

Leaving Oneida in June 1879, John Humphrey Noyes remained in Canada, gathering a small community of older members who wished to remain true to the old principles on a smaller scale. The remnants of the kingdom of heaven on earth lived out their lives at Niagara Falls under Noyes's guidance, adhering to the tenets of Bible communism without its radical sexual practices. After his death in 1886, Noyes's body was returned to Oneida for burial. The Oneida Community did try to revive its religious beliefs, but, failing to do so, it ultimately established itself as a totally secular economic entity. Today, Oneida, Ltd. manufactures silver and stainless-steel tableware less than a mile from the Mansion House.

9

Epilogue

Consistency between the "real" and "ideal" is the heart of the utopian promise. For religiously inspired utopian experiments this means a sacred order on earth; for nineteenth-century Protestant American religious utopians it meant a literal kingdom of heaven on earth. We have looked at the Oneida Community as one example of the utopian attempt to transcend the tension between religious ideals and the social, cultural, and economic orders of the world. We have also looked at the first and second Great Awakenings as, in part, religious responses to the tension between religion and world, and as failures in fully resolving or transcending those tensions. It would be a mistake to conclude that we have exposed a general trend toward valuative and normative consistency in American religious history. While many were deeply moved by revivalism and radically altered their religious and worldly activity, many were opposed to the "new measures" or unexcited by them. Of those awakened by revivalism, only a few were so compelled by its failure to unify religion and world to take the further utopian steps. The vast majority were fully capable of holding the contradictory impulses of the sacred and secular spheres. The leap into utopia, then, was taken by a small number of religious enthusiasts who found in the intractability of the world the warrant for more radical steps.

Among the Oneida communists the tension between religion and world was transcended by questioning and revising the Christian tradition. The judgment of the Jews and the destruction of Jerusalem's Temple at the hands of the Romans in A.D. 70 marked the Second Coming and the end of a complete religious era. The new dispensation promised secure salvation and freedom from sin. The judgment of the Jewish era made possible the kingdom of heaven on earth, and salvation and perfection in this life. Religion and world were no longer separate spheres—they had been merged theoretically and practically.

Formal religious law, appropriate for the earlier eras, became superfluous once the law was engraved in the heart of the spiritually cleansed. Inspiration—not law, custom, or tradition—provided the blueprint for the earthly kingdom of heaven, and the progressive nature of perfection provided the license for radical institutional change and individual development. The Oneida Community, led by Christ's true representative and composed of those perfect in faith, was to be the vanguard of that kingdom. Religious truth and communal success would convince the world to abandon its anachronistic religion, social relations, and institutions. Noyes's success at transcending the tensions between religion and world theologically made for an innovative family structure and a dynamic intellectual and economic life. For all that, amidst Oneida's success, new tensions emerged.

The formation of a separate community shifted the boundary between religion and world. Sacred and secular had been merged within the community, but the boundary between religion and world shifted to the interface of in-group/out-group.

Science had not been a problem for the Bible communists at the inception of communal life. Until the 1850s many saw science and religion fitting hand in glove. Science gave people the opportunity to explore the depths of the physical world and better understand God's work. Rather than dismissing or refuting religion, science offered rational explanations for Scripture and revelation, hence providing deeper knowledge. Only when science began to compete with religion, offering explanations that challenged Scripture and revelation, did science become problematic for the Oneida Community. Perhaps the debate raging between science and religion would have passed over the Oneida Community if its youth had not been sent into the world for higher education, or if secular knowledge had been devalued. Once the younger community members returned from college with worldly scientific rationalism and religious skepticism, the external debate had been brought into the community. Just as pious scientists and theologians had gone to great lengths to protect religion from scientific debunking and failed, John Humphrey Noyes could not protect Perfectionism from the imported positivist challenge. Because the tenets of religion could not be proved scientifically, the tension between the two could not be overcome. As Dr. Theodore Noyes discovered, it could only be bracketed: the most that could be done was to agree to suspend the argument to save the community from divisiveness. To expel the young disbelievers would have meant writing off the most talented of their generation and giving up hope for the reconversion. Outspoken unbelievers withdrew of their own accord, leaving the shadow of their skepticism behind.

Democratic theocracy was plausible only as far as there existed consensus on the principles of Perfectionism and the inspiration of John Humphrey Noyes. If belief in either flagged, the delicate balance would be tipped and either theocracy or democracy would ascend as the means of legitimate authority. The declining influence of John Humphrey Noyes and the religious doubt or unbelief of a significant segment of the community left a power vacuum within which factions crystallized and competed.

Complex marriage resolved the tension between religion and world in regard to sex and the family, but second-order tensions emerged on another level. Sublimated sexual rivalry and jealousy raised conflict over ascending fellowship and ultimately over the leadership of the community itself. Tension between sex and religion reemerged as conflict over sexual privileges and prerogatives within complex marriage.

Tension between religion and world in the economic sphere had been transcended through Perfectionist justifications. The very same justifications that made economic prosperity possible required the community industries to be run more and more on a rational, profit-oriented basis. With economic growth and diversity, inspiration and community input had to be replaced with cold calculation and managerial exclusiveness. The surfacing of these second-order tensions between religion and world drained the utopian optimism of the Oneida Community and turned its attention to compromises that would keep the community intact and its members from the clutches of the outside world. Oneida became less a value-based community, and more a community whose preeminent value was "community."

We have seen the conflict of sacred and secular orders providing a

point of departure for the religious innovations of the Great Awakenings and the Oneida Community. The Great Awakenings stimu-
lated religious interest and church membership, providing a spring-
board for the religiously predisposed who swelled the ranks of
utopian sects. The utopian character of reformulated sacred histories
and prophecy—and here we are using "utopian" in Mannheim's
sense—was used by the Shakers, Millerites, and the Oneida Community, among others, to span the chasm separating religion and world,
providing theological justification for utopian renovations of culture, institutions, and social relations. Once the tidal wave of religious excitement recedes and the calmer currents of everyday life are
restored, we find new contiguities of religion and world presenting
new tensions. For the Oneida Community these second-order tensions proved insurmountable within the confines of religious
community.

The case of the Oneida Community demonstrates the stubborn re-
assertion of tension between religion and world despite the apparent
success of transcending sacred histories. Oneida Perfectionism was
much more flexible and dynamic than most other utopian theologies,
yet was still not elastic enough. This suggests that the success of religious utopias depends, in part, upon periodic renewals of religious
enthusiasm that renovate theology, shatter the utopian institutional
structure, and restore the charismatic community capable of transcending the new tensions.

Restoring the health of an ailing utopian community is difficult.
First, a new charismatic leader—or a revived old one—may be required to shatter the everyday routine and legitimate the new utopian order. Second, the community's reason for being depends upon
the first surge of enthusiasm, the first leader, and the original religious promise. The revolution within utopia requires recognition of
its failure, and the failure of the utopian's life work. We must remember that utopias absorb all the individual's energies and commitment. The utopian may very well be unprepared, unwilling, or unable to recognize his or her total failure and cling to the reaffirming,
"old" utopian ways. Third, failure may deflate optimism, generating
defections and divisiveness, which makes the new leap into utopia
even more difficult. Fourth, the new utopian order must be able to
reproduce itself not only biologically, but ideologically as well. The
first generation of utopians had an external world to reject, reformu-
late, and revolutionize, and had to form the basis for commitment

and community. For them, utopia is problematic: for the second generation utopia may be taken for granted. Without a primary commitment to world-rejection, second-generation utopians may lack the solidarity and motivations characteristic of the original intentional community and require new ideological underpinning to legitimate utopian life. Fifth, utopian experiments have, for the most part, arisen out of wider social, cultural, and economic contexts that make utopia seem inviting, plausible, and potentially successful. If the wider social environment does not open these avenues to utopian experiments it will be difficult for the struggling utopia to hold disaffected members or attract new ones.

The formation of a utopian religious community bent on transforming the world holds out the promise of an earthly order that conforms to an other-worldly sacred design. The cleavage between religious and secular order must be fused into a transcendent whole. This was the scheme of the Shakers and Mormons in their utopian phase, as well as the Oneida Community. Utopian transcendence can only be maintained on a theoretical level. The utopian community is still "in the world," alongside the outside world, and its members are only would-be and aspiring saints. Utopian institutions may very well transcend the tensions between religion and world, but they are still worldly institutions that provide the locus for new tensions between religion and world.

The evangelical mission of religious utopias locks the utopian community into a particular relationship with the world: as a collective emissary or exemplary prophet pointing the way to heaven on earth. The boundary beween heaven and earth, heretofore between this world and the other world, becomes a physical boundary between utopia and extopia. Radically new forms of social relations and institutional activity become the targets of outsiders who may be morally threatened or offended by utopian forms, or possessed of a competing vision of religion, utopia, and its prospects for manifestation on earth. Finally, unless the utopian community can successfully isolate its members from the culture of the outside world, external developments may offer other compelling visions or worldviews—such as science or the outside conventions themselves—and provide the basis for utopia-rejecting rather than world-rejecting ideologies. The Oneida Community established new utopian boundaries between religion and world, and new tensions between these spheres peculiar to religious utopia developed. The literary license available to fictional utopians allows absolute separation of the utopian from the nonutopian world. Religious utopias lack this advantage because they are both outside the world and of the world, and they suffer the conflicts generated at the utopian boundary between religion and world.

Notes

1   Introduction

1   Rosabeth Moss Kanter, "Commitment and Social Organization: A Study of Commitment Mechanisms in Utopian Communities," *American Sociological Review* 33 (August 1968): 499–517. In her later, extended treatment of utopian communities, *Commitment and Community: Communes and Utopias in Sociological Perspective* (Cambridge: Harvard University Press, 1972), Kanter discusses the deterioration of commitment, but chiefly in terms of formal organization, i.e., the consequences of disasters, debts and disagreement, the changing external environment, aging of core members and the problems of youth and recruitment, the conflict between religious values and economic and political needs, and the impact of prosperity. Kanter thus broaches our subject, but does not pursue it very far.

2   Karen H. Stephan and G. E. Stephan, "Religion and the Survival of Utopian Communities," *Journal for the Scientific Study of Religion* 12 (March 1973): 89–100, quotation from p. 93.

3   Harry B. Hawthorne, "Utopias and Durability in Literature and Reality," *International Journal of Comparative Sociology* 4 (March 1963): 50–56.

4   Marin Lockwood Carden, *Oneida: Utopian Community to Modern Corporation* (New York: Harper and Row, 1969), pp. 89–91.

5   Constance Noyes Robertson, *Oneida Community: The Breakup, 1876–1881* (Syracuse: Syracuse University Press, 1972).

6   Max Weber, *From Max Weber: Essays in Sociology*, ed. and trans. H. H. Gerth and C. Wright Mills (New York: Oxford University Press, 1946), pp. 323–59.

7   Ibid., p. 323.

8   See Carden, *Oneida*; Lewis A. Coser, "Greedy Organizations," *European Journal of Sociology* 8 (October 1967): 196–215; Allan Estlake, *The Oneida Community: A Record of an Attempt to Carry Out the Principles of Christian Unselfishness and Scientific Race-Improvement* (1900; reprint ed., New York: AMS Press, 1973); Robert S. Fogarty, "Oneida: A Utopian Search for Religious Security," *Labor History* 14 (Spring 1973); Mark Holloway, *Heavens on Earth: Utopian Communities in America, 1680–1880* (New York: Dover Publications, 1966); Pierrepont Noyes, *My Father's House: An Oneida Boyhood* (New York: Farrar and Rinehart, 1937); Spencer C. Olin, Jr., "The Oneida Community and the Instability of Charismatic Authority," *Journal of American History* 67 (September 1980): 285–300; and Robertson, *Oneida Community: The Breakup.*

9   Benjamin Nelson, "Max Weber, Ernst Troeltsch, George Jellinek as Comparative Historical Sociologists, *Sociological Analysis* 36 (1975): 229–40.

10   Weber, *From Max Weber*, p. 280.

11   Ernest Lee Tuveson, *Millennium and Utopia: A Study in the Background of the Idea of Progress* (New York: Harper and Row, Harper Torchbooks, 1964).

12   Weber, *From Max Weber*, p. 328.

13   Georg Simmel, *Conflict and the Web of Group Affiliations*, trans. Kurt H. Wolff and Reinhard Bendix (New York: The Free Press, 1955), pp. 150–58.

14   John Humphrey Noyes, *The Religious Experience of John Humphrey Noyes, Founder of the Oneida Community*, ed. George Wallingford Noyes (New York: Macmillan Co., 1923), pp. 69–89; Oneida Community, *Handbook of the Oneida Community, 1867 and 1871, Bound with Mutual Criticism* (The 1867 and 1871 editions of *The Handbook*, Wallingford, Connecticut: Office of the Circular, Wallingford Community; and Oneida, New York: Oneida Community, respectively; the 1876 edition of *Mutual Criticism*, Oneida, New York: Office of the American Socialist; reprint, New York: AMS Press, 1976), pp. 31–53. By 1871 Noyes had lengthened his list of reasons to seventeen.

15   John H. Noyes, *The Berean: A Manual for the Help of Those Who Seek the Faith of the Primitive Church* (Putney, Vt: Office of the Spiritual Magazine, 1847); cited in John McKelvie Whitworth, *God's Blueprint: A Sociological Study of Three Utopian Sects* (London: Routledge and Kegan Paul, 1975), p. 101. The *Berean* was a collection of Noyes's early writings and reflected his theological development to this point. He later reformulated this scheme without changing any of the essentials. The first era became the "natural state," the second, the "legal state," the third, the "spiritual state," and the fourth, the "glorified state," a postregenerative era. The period from Christ to Noyes and the era of rapid spiritual development in the earlier formulation had been merged. See Oneida Community, *Handbook and Mutual Criticism*, p. 40.

16   Noyes, *Religious Experience*, p. 89.

17   Alfred Barron and George Noyes Miller, eds., *Home-Talks by John Humphrey Noyes* (Oneida, N.Y.: Wallingford Printing Co., 1875), vol. 1, quoted in Carden, *Oneida*, p. 15.

18   Oneida Community, *Handbook and Mutual Criticism* (1871), pp. 46–48.

19   Weber, *From Max Weber*, p. 323.

20   Carden, *Oneida*, pp. 23–24.

21 John M. Janzen, "Deep Thought: Structure and Intention in Kongo Prophetism 1910–1921," *Social Research* 46 (Spring 1979): 138.

2 The Tension between Religion and Economy

1 E. Digby Baltzell, *Puritan Boston and Quaker Philadelphia: Two Protestant Ethics and the Spirit of Class Authority and Leadership* (New York: The Free Press, 1979); Charles A. Barker, *American Convictions: Cycles of Public Thought, 1600–1850* (Philadelphia and New York: J. B. Lippincott, 1970); Roland Bertoff, *An Unsettled People: Social Order and Disorder in American History* (New York: Harper and Row, 1971); Stuart Bruchey, *The Roots of American Economic Growth, 1607–1861: An Essay in Social Causation* (New York: Harper and Row, 1965); J. E. Crowley, *This Sheba, Self: The Conceptualization of Economic Life in Eighteenth-Century America* (Baltimore: Johns Hopkins University Press, 1974); Joseph Dorfman, *The Economic Mind in American Civilization, 1606–1865*, 2 vols. (New York: Viking Press, 1946); Gabriel Kolko, "Max Weber on America: Theory and Evidence," *History and Theory* 1 (1961); Perry Miller, *The New England Mind: The Seventeenth Century* (Cambridge: Harvard University Press, 1954), pp. 40–52; Perry Miller, *The Life of the Mind in America: From the Revolution to the Civil War* (New York: Harcourt, Brace and World, 1965). See also: Max Lerner, *America as a Civilization* (New York: Simon and Schuster, 1957); Henry F. May, *Protestant Churches and Industrial America* (New York: Harper and Row, 1949); Vernon Lewis Parrington, *Main Currents in American Thought*, 3 vols. (New York: Harcourt, Brace and World, 1927), vol. 1, *The Colonial Mind, 1620–1800*; Thorstein Veblen, "Christian Morals and the Competitive System," *International Journal of Ethics* 20 (January 1910), reprinted in Thorstein Veblen, *Essays in Our Changing Order*, ed. Leon Ardzrooni (New York: Viking Press, 1954). See Weber, "Religious Rejections of the World and Their Directions," in *From Max Weber*, pp. 323–59.

2 Weber, *From Max Weber*, p. 331.

3 Miller, *New England Mind: The Seventeenth Century*, p. 4.

4 Ibid., pp. 27–40, 307.

5 William Perkins, "A Treatise of the Vocations," in *The Works of . . . William Perkins* (Cambridge, 1605), cited in Crowley, *This Sheba, Self*, p. 54; John Cotton, excerpts from *A Way of Life* (London, 1641), reprinted in *The Puritans*, ed. Perry Miller and Thomas H. Johnson (New York: American Book Co., 1938), pp. 319–24.

6 Miller, *New England Mind: The Seventeenth Century*, p. 44. Arminianism's fundamental doctrine was freedom of the will. The elect were not prechosen; those who lived a righteous and virtuous life could bring themselves closer to salvation. The path to salvation began with an assertion of will and positive achievement. See Parrington, *Main Currents*, 1: 152–54.

7 Miller, *New England Mind: The Seventeenth Century*, pp. 53–67.

8 Max Weber, *The Protestant Ethic and the Spirit of Capitalism* (New York: Charles Scribner's Sons, 1958), p. 80.

9 See Bertoff, *Unsettled People*; Crowley, *This Sheba, Self*; Richard Hofstadter, *Anti-Intellectualism in American Life* (New York: Random House, 1963); William G. McLoughlin, *Revivals, Awakenings, and Reform: An Essay on Social*

Change in America, 1607–1977 (Chicago: University of Chicago Press, 1978);
Sidney E. Mead, "The Rise of the Evangelical Conception of the Ministry in America:
1607–1859," in *The Ministry in Historical Perspective*, ed. H. Richard Niebuhr and
Daniel D. Williams (New York: Harper and Brothers, 1959), pp. 207–49; Perry
Miller, *The New England Mind: From Colony to Province* (Cambridge: Harvard University Press, 1953), and *New England Mind: The Seventeenth Century*; Parrington,
Main Currents, vol. 1; Harvey Wish, *Society and Thought in Early America: A Social
and Intellectual History of the American People through 1865* (New York: David
McKay, 1950); and the works of the revivalists themselves, especially Jonathan
Edwards.

10   Robert E. Brown, *Middle-Class Democracy and Revolution in Massachusetts,
1691–1780* (Ithaca: Cornell University Press, 1955), pp. 62–68.

11   Parrington, *Main Currents*, 2:44. Also see Douglas C. North, *The Economic
Growth of the United States, 1790–1860* (Englewood Cliffs, N.J.: Prentice Hall,
1961): 156–77 on the industrial development of the Northeast.

12   Rolla Milton Tryon, *Household Manufacturers in the United States, 1640–1860*
(1917; reprint, New York: August M. Kelly, 1966), is still the definitive study of the
transformation from household to factory manufacturing.

13   Bruchey, *American Economic Growth*, pp. 50–53; Crowley, *This Sheba, Self*,
p. 12.

14   Herbert G. Gutman, "Work, Culture, and Society in Industrializing America,
1815–1919," *American Historical Review* 78 (June 1973): 531–88; E. P. Thompson, "Time, Work-Discipline, and Industrial Capitalism," *Past and Present* 38 (December 1967): 56–97.

15   Dorfman, *Economic Mind*, 2:620.

16   The labor literature of the time variously attacked technology, chartered monopolistic banks, mercantile speculation, inheritance laws, monied aristocracy and priestly hierarchy, high rents and poor housing, usury laws, poor laws, company stores,
long hours for women and children, class divisions (a particular target of German immigrants and English Chartists), and private property. It variously favored universal
education, banks owned by small shareholders, machine technology, land reform,
new agrarianism, communal possession of property, and a host of other reforms arising from the abuses they opposed. See ibid., 637–95.

17   U.S. Bureau of the Census, *Historical Statistics of the United States: Colonial
Times to 1970*, 2 vols., pt. 2, Bicentennial Edition (Washington, D.C.: U.S. Government Printing Office, 1975), 1:8–11.

18   Douglas C. North, *The Economic Growth of the United States, 1790–1860*
(Englewood Cliffs, N.J.: Prentice Hall, 1961), pp. 55–57; Wish, *Society and Thought*,
pp. 399–400.

19   Dorfman, *Economic Mind*, 2:517–19.

20   See Charles C. Cole, Jr., *The Social Ideas of the Northern Evangelists, 1826–
1860* (New York: Octagon Books, 1977): 179–83; Dorfman, *Economic Mind*, pp.
758–66; May, *Protestant Churches*, pp. 14–15.

21   Cole, *Social Ideas of Northern Evangelists*, pp. 164–65.

22   Ibid.

23 Albert Barnes, "Revivals of Religion in Cities and Large Towns," *American National Preacher* 15 (1841): 23, quoted by Cole, *Social Ideas of Northern Evangelists*, p. 167.

24 See John L. Hammond, *The Politics of Benevolence: Revival Religion and American Voting Behavior* (Norwood, N. J.: Ablex Publishing, 1979), on the political support for abolitionism and antislavery in the revival areas of Ohio and New York State.

3 *Religion and Democracy*

1 Weber, *From Max Weber*, pp. 333–40.

2 Ralph H. Gabriel, *The Course of American Democratic Thought: An Intellectual History Since 1815* (New York: Ronald Press, 1956), p. 14. This section will draw heavily on this book, pp. 3–39.

3 Quoted in ibid., p. 17.

4 See Tuveson, *Millennium and Utopia*, for an extended treatment of this theme.

5 Gabriel, *American Democratic Thought*, p. 23.

6 Michael Zuckerman, "The Social Context of Democracy in Massachusetts," *William and Mary Quarterly*, 2d ser., 25 (October 1968): 523–44.

7 See Mead, "Rise of the Evangelical Conception of the Ministry," pp. 207–49; Seymour Martin Lipset, "Religion and Politics in the American Past and Present," in *Religion and Social Conflict*, ed. Robert Lee and Martin E. Marty (New York: Oxford University Press, 1964), pp. 72–76; and Ralph Barton Perry, *Puritanism and Democracy* (New York: Vanguard Press, 1944), pp. 104–10, 187–96, on Episcopal, Congregational, and Presbyterian modes of organization and democracy.

8 The following discussion of Thomas Hooker, John Cotton, and Anne Hutchinson is based upon Miller, *New England Mind: From Colony to Province*, pp. 56–67.

9 Perry Miller, "Jonathan Edwards' Sociology of the Great Awakening," *New England Quarterly* 21 (March 1948): 50–77.

10 Jonathan Edwards, *The Works of Jonathan Edwards*, 4 vols. (New Haven: Yale University Press, 1957–1975), vol. 1, *Freedom of the Will*, ed. Paul Ramsey (1957); vol. 4, *The Great Awakening*, ed. C. C. Goen (1972); Jonathan Edwards, *Representative Selections*, ed. Clarence H. Faust and Thomas H. Johnson, rev. ed. (New York: Hill and Wang, 1962). See also Barker, *American Convictions*, pp. 172–80; Parrington, *Main Currents*, 1:151–65.

11 Charles Grandison Finney, quoted in William G. McLoughlin, Jr., *Modern Revivalism: Charles Grandison Finney to Billy Graham* (New York: Ronald Press, 1959), p. 25. The following discussion of Finney's thought owes much to this work.

12 Hammond, *Politics of Benevolence*. Finney unequivocally embraced the temperance movement and various attempts at moral, political, and business reform, but supported abolitionism only reluctantly when his supporters threatened to leave him behind on the issue. As we have already seen, revival leaders most often shied away from tampering with the institutional relations of economy and society and tended to reduce social problems to moral deficiencies.

13 Lyman Beecher, *Works*, vol. 1, *Lectures on Political Atheism and Kindred Sub-*

jects, Together with Six Lectures on Intemperance (Boston, 1852), pp. 91–139, quoted in May, *Protestant Churches*, p. 9.

14 This section on antimasonry relies heavily on Whitney R. Cross, *The Burned-Over District: The Social and Intellectual History of Enthusiastic Religion in Western New York, 1800–1850* (1950; reprint, New York: Harper Torchbooks, 1965), pp. 113–25.

15 Dixon Ryan Fox, *The Decline of Aristocracy in the Politics of New York, 1801–1840,* ed. Robert V. Remini (1919; reprint ed., New York: Harper and Row, 1965), pp. 53–54.

16 Robert Troup to Rufus King, quoted in Fox, *Decline of Aristocracy in New York,* p. 137, 139.

17 See Alvin Kass, *Politics in New York State, 1800–1830* (Syracuse: Syracuse University Press, 1965), pp. 1–24, for a detailed discussion of the "soap operatic" party intrigue and maneuvering of the period.

18 George Bancroft, *History of the United States of America, From the Founding of the Continent,* 6 vols. (New York: D. Appleton, 1883–1885), 1: 1, quoted in Fox, *Decline of Aristocracy in New York,* p. 249.

19 See Kass, *Politics in New York State,* pp. 73–92; and Fox, *Decline of Aristocracy in New York,* pp. 229–70, for the detailed debates of the convention.

20 *Report of the Proceedings and Debates of the Convention of 1821* (Albany, 1821), p. 219; quoted by Fox, *Decline of Aristocracy in New York,* p. 251.

21 Fox, *Decline of Aristocracy in New York,* p. 274.

4   The Tension between Religion and Sex, Women, and the Family

1 Stanford M. Lyman, *The Seven Deadly Sins: Society and Evil* (New York: St. Martin's Press, 1978), pp. 54–59.

2 Ibid., p. 80.

3 Milton Rugoff, *Prudery and Passion* (New York: G. P. Putnam's Sons, 1971), p. 26. In addition to political, philosophical, economic, and scientific tracts and almanacs, Franklin occasionally delved into erotica without abandoning the reason, rationalism, and calculation that made him—for Max Weber—the embodiment of the modern capitalist spirit. His most famous piece in this genre, "Advice to a Young Man on Choosing a Mistress," recommended older women because there would be no danger of children or ruin, and because they were experienced, discreet, indistinguishable below the waist from a young woman, and more grateful. We see in these thoughts the method of the successful entrepreneur: maximize profit in pleasure and safety, and minimize loss in risk and the appearance of impropriety. See also Carl Degler, "What Ought to Be and What Was: Women's Sexuality in the Nineteenth Century," *American Historical Review* 79 (December 1974): 1467–90.

4 See Arthur W. Calhoun, *A Social History of the American Family: From Colonial Times to the Present,* 3 vols. in one (New York: Barnes and Noble, 1945), 1:22–45. See also Morton M. Hunt, *The Natural History of Love* (New York: Funk and Wagnalls Publishing Co., 1959), pp. 220–31, for Luther's and Calvin's attitudes toward sex and marriage.

5   Quoted by Hunt, *The Natural History of Love*, pp. 223–24.

6   Edmund S. Morgan, *The Puritan Family: Religion and Domestic Relations in Seventeenth-Century New England* (New York: Harper and Row, 1966); and "The Puritans and Sex," *New England Quarterly* (December 1942): 591–607, reprinted in *The American Family in Social-Historical Perspective*, ed. Michael Gordon (New York: St. Martin's Press, 1973), pp. 282–95.

7   Hunt, *Natural History of Love*, p. 252.

8   Lyman, *Seven Deadly Sins*, pp. 75–76.

9   See Calhoun, *American Family*, 1:129–51, on public sexual confessions and the Puritan church.

10   William I. Thomas, *Sex and Society: Studies in the Social Psychology of Sex*, 6th ed. (Boston: Gorham Press, 1907), pp. 115–16.

11   Degler, "What Ought to Be."

12   Charles E. Rosenberg, "Sexuality, Class and Role in Nineteenth-Century America," *American Quarterly* 25 (May 1973): 131–53; Ben Barker-Benfield, "The Spermatic Economy: A Nineteenth-Century View of Sexuality," *Feminist Studies* 1 (Summer 1972): 45–75. Eventually the Zoarites and Ephratans tolerated monogamy as a lesser alternative if celibacy could not be maintained.

13   Rupert, Vermont, Congregational Church, "Fornication Binds the Criminal Parties to Marry, the decision of the Congregational Church in Rupert, Vermont relative to a case of discipline. The result of an Ecclesiastical Council, convened in that place August 31, 1814. A dissertation delivered on the occasion by one of the council, a letter of admonition addressed to the offender, and the form of excommunication. With an appendix, containing strictures on fornication and divorcement" (Bennington, Vt., 1815).

14   Ibid., pp. 14, 18.

15   Barbara J. Harris, *Beyond Her Sphere: Women and the Professions in American History*, Contributions in Women's Studies, no. 4 (Westport, Conn.: Greenwood Press, 1978), pp. 3–19.

16   John Milton, *Paradise Lost*, bk. 4, lines 295–301, quoted in Hunt, *Natural History of Love*, p. 249.

17   Barbara Welter, "The Cult of True Womanhood: 1820–1860," *American Quarterly* 18 (Summer 1966): 151–74.

18   See Carroll Smith-Rosenberg, "The Hysterical Woman: Sex Roles and Role Conflict in 19th Century America," *Social Research* 39 (Winter 1972): 656–59; and Welter, "Cult of True Womanhood," p. 174.

19   Calhoun, *American Family*, 2:93–97, 126–29.

20   Ibid., 1:43–45.

21   See Morgan, *Puritan Family*, p. 133.

22   See above, chapter 2, "The Tension between Religion and Economy."

23   See Calhoun, *American Family*, 1:146–49.

24   Alexis de Tocqueville, *Democracy in America*, ed. Phillip Bradley, 2 vols. (New York: Alfred A. Knopf, 1945), 2:194.

25 Tocqueville and other foreign observers noticed that before marriage American women enjoyed a measure of freedom that surpassed their European counterparts. Upon marriage the independence of women was irrevocably lost.

26 The following will serve only as an introduction to Noyes's sexual and familial ideology. These themes will be given more extensive treatment in chapter 6, "The Theology of John Humphrey Noyes," and chapter 7, "The Oneida Community: Transcending the Tension between Religion and World in Practice."

27 See John H. Noyes, "Home-Talk," in Barron and Miller, *Home-Talks*, pp. 14–23.

5 The Tension between Religion and Science

1 The stirpiculture program will be examined in detail in chapters 7 and 8.

2 Weber, *From Max Weber*, pp. 350, 351.

3 Max Weber, *Economy and Society: An Outline of Interpretative Sociology*, ed. Guenther Roth and Claus Wittich, 2 vols. (Berkeley: University of California Press, 1978), 1:500–501, 503–5.

4 Benjamin Franklin, "Articles of Belief and Acts of Religion," (1728), cited by Barker, *American Convictions*, pp. 213–14.

5 See Robert K. Merton, *Science, Technology and Society in Seventeenth-Century England* (1938; reprint, New York: Howard Fertig, 1970).

6 Brooke Hindle, "The Quaker Background and Science in Colonial Philadelphia," *Isis* 46, pt. 3 (September 1955): 243–50; Baltzell, *Boston and Philadelphia*, pp. 169–75.

7 Theodore Dwight Bozeman, *Protestants in an Age of Science: The Baconian Ideal and Antebellum American Religious Thought* (Chapel Hill: University of North Carolina Press, 1977).

8 George H. Daniels, *American Science in the Age of Jackson* (New York: Columbia University Press, 1968), pp. 51–53.

9 See Znaniecki, *The Social Role of the Man of Knowledge* (New York: Harper and Row, 1940), pp. 14–15; and Robert K. Merton, *The Sociology of Science: Theoretical and Empirical Investigations*, ed. Norman W. Storer (Chicago: University of Chicago Press, 1973), pp. 34–46, on the concept of the "social circle" and the sociology of knowledge.

10 Edward Hitchcock, "The Relations and Mutual Duties between the Philosopher and Theologian," *Bibliotheca Sacra* 10 (1853): 191–92, 194; reprinted in Edward Hitchcock, *Religious Truth, Illustrated from Science* (Boston, 1857), pp. 54–97; quoted in Daniels, *American Science*, pp. 51–52.

11 James Dwight Dana, "Science and the Bible," *Bibliotheca Sacra* 13 (January 1856): 81; cited by Daniels, *American Science*, pp. 55–58.

12 Dirk Struik, *The Origins of American Science (New England)* (New York: Cameron Associates, 1957), pp. 29–30.

13 Ibid., p. 277.

14 Daniels, *American Science*, pp. 118–19.

15 Early nineteenth-century science held "theory" to be a simple generalization from facts. Rather than conceptual statements, "theory" included a great number of facts of the same nature. A theory had to be judged true or false before it could be evaluated for its utility. That this is not strongly insisted upon in modern physics indicates a radically different conception of theory and a shift in the kinds of data considered. "Quarks," "quasars," "neutrinos," and electron "spin" required a significant transformation in what is meant by "observation," from the readily observable scientific work of an earlier era. Combustion, tangible bodies in motion (be they proximate or distant), the morphology of flora and fauna, and the color, hardness, texture, and weight of minerals were direct observations requiring only a sharp eye, simple instruments, and a knowledge of the regnant classification system. Hypothesis was not given even a limited role, as it seemed to be an application of assumed rules rather than "hard facts." The atomic theory of chemistry was suspect in its early years because of its "hypothetical" nature. It was accepted because of its obvious utility, but suspect, nonetheless.

16 Francis Wayland—clergyman, educator, philosopher, and political economist— elegantly espouses this normative basis for scientific epistemology in his "Discourse on the Philosophy of Analogy." He was strongly influenced by second Great Awakening revivalism, but the "divine" basis of analogical reasoning was not embraced by evangelical Christians alone. Benjamin Pierce, the renowned nineteenth-century American mathematician, expressed similar sentiments. See Daniels, *American Science*, pp. 167–70, 173–74.

17 Richard H. Shyrock, "American Indifference to Basic Science during the Nineteenth Century," *Archives Internationales d'Histoire des Sciences* 28 (October 1948): 50–65.

18 Hofstadter, *Anti-Intellectualism*, pp. 53–57.

19 Jeremiah Reynolds to President Andrew Jackson, 16 November 1836, reprinted in *Science in Nineteenth-Century America: A Documentary History*, ed. Nathan Reingold (New York: Hill and Wang, 1964), pp. 112–18.

20 Miller, *Life of the Mind*, p. 283. Of course there were exceptions to American scientific mediocrity in the eighteenth century. Governor John Winthrop, Jr., of Massachusetts, and Cotton Mather were both early members of the Royal Society and, later, such luminaries as Professor John Winthrop of Harvard and Benjamin Franklin joined the ranks of "Friends of the Royal Society." Recognition, however, did not reduce the distance from the European centers of scientific growth. Except for small clusters of enthusiasts in or near Philadelphia and Boston, colonial scientists were isolated. They corresponded with each other and with scientists overseas, but for the most part they worked alone. American isolation did encourage certain kinds of scientific activity. Exploration, geographical surveys, map-making, and Indian studies abounded, and the Crown regularly demanded reports on population, natural resources, and areas of economic promise from colonial governors. Southern science was equally isolated, decentralized, and imitative of Europe.

21 Hindle, "Quaker Background," p. 244; Baltzell, *Boston and Philadelphia*; Barker, *American Convictions*, p. 376.

22 Silliman suggested that there might be a long period between creation's "in the beginning" and the Genetic six days. James Dwight Dana refused to be put on the defensive by the "literalists" and theologians: he defended the conclusions of science, but

attacked the "literalists" in defense of religion. The "literalists" not only did a disservice to the Bible, they also led people to believe that science and religion were hostile. In such a state of mind, one might give up the Bible altogether! See Struik, *Origins of American Science*, pp 302–4.

23   Asa Gray, "Review of Darwin's Theory on the *Origins of Species* By Means of Natural Selection," *American Journal of Science and Arts* 2d ser., 24 (March 1860): 156.

24   Ibid., pp. 160–61.

25   Mead, "Rise of the Evangelical Conception of the Ministry," pp. 207–49.

6   *The Theology of John Humphrey Noyes*

1   Ernest Lee Tuveson, *Redeemer Nation: The Idea of America's Millennial Role* (Chicago: University of Chicago Press, 1968), pp. 129–30.

2   Quoted in McLoughlin, *Modern Revivalism*, pp. 101–4; from Charles Grandison Finney, *Lectures on Systematic Theology* (Oberlin, 1878); *Sermons on Various Subjects* (New York, 1833), or *Lectures on Revivals of Religion* (New York, 1832).

3   Tuveson, *Millennium and Utopia*, passim, and *Redeemer Nation*, pp. 26–51.

4   Karl Mannheim, *Ideology and Utopia: An Introduction to the Sociology of Knowledge*, trans. Louis Wirth and Edward Shils (New York: Harcourt, Brace and World, 1936), p. 192.

5   John McKelvie Whitworth, *God's Blueprint*, pp. 17–22.

6   Noyes, *Religious Experience*, p. 110.

7   John H. Noyes, *The Doctrine of Salvation from Sin, Explained and Defended* (Putney, Vt., 1843), pp. 22–23.

8   John Humphrey Noyes, *Religious Experience*, pp. 181–82.

9   Noyes traveled to New York City to read William L. Garrison his declaration. Garrison published it, without attribution, in his periodical, *Liberator*, October 1837; quoted in Whitworth, *God's Blueprint*, pp. 94–95.

10   John H. Noyes, "Democratic Theocracy," *American Socialist*, 8 May 1879 (originally published in 1844).

11   John Humphrey Noyes, *History of American Socialisms* (1870; reprint, New York: Hillary House, 1961); *American Socialist*, 30 March 1876–25 December 1879.

12   Noyes, *History of American Socialisms*, pp. 26–27.

13   *Circular*, 28 November 1870, p. 293; quoted in Richard DeMaria, *Communal Love at Oneida: A Perfectionist Vision of Authority, Property, and Sexual Order* (New York: Edwin Mellen Press, 1978), p. 51.

14   *Circular*, 17 February 1859, p. 13; in DeMaria, *Communal Love at Oneida*, p. 74. See pp. 50–78 on the Oneida Community's concept of true love.

15   *Circular*, 31 May 1860, p. 71; quoted in ibid., p. 61 n.

16   Quoted in Constance Noyes Robertson, *Oneida Community Profiles* (Syracuse: Syracuse University Press, 1977), p. 21.

17   It may seem hypocritical for the author of the *Battle Axe* letter to confine himself in marriage. Propriety and appearance were certainly important in Noyes's desire to marry, but his letter of proposal, written 11 June 1838 to Harriet Holten, reveals his convictions. Since in heaven there is no marriage, "we can enter into no engagements with each other which shall limit the range of affections as they are limited in matrimonial engagements by the fashion of this world. I desire and expect my yoke-fellow will love all who love God, whether man or woman, with a warmth and strength of affection which is unknown to earthly lovers, and freely as if she stood in no particular connection with me." Noyes also assured Harriet he would neither monopolize nor enslave her heart. Quoted in Robert Allerton Parker, *A Yankee Saint: John Humphrey Noyes and the Oneida Community* (New York: G. P. Putnam's Sons, 1935), pp. 59–60.

7   *The Oneida Community: Transcending the Tensions between Religion and World in Practice*

1   For histories of the Oneida Community see Carden, *Oneida*; Estlake, *The Oneida Community*; P. Noyes, *My Father's House*; Parker, *A Yankee Saint*; Constance Noyes Robertson, *Oneida Community: An Autobiography, 1851–1876* (Syracuse: Syracuse University Press, 1970); and Robertson, *Oneida Community: The Breakup.*

2   George Wallingford Noyes, "Episodes in the Life of John Humphrey Noyes," *Community Quadrangle* 2 (December 1927): 6; quoted in Carden, *Oneida*, p. 45.

3   Oneida Community, *First Annual Report of the Oneida Association: Exhibiting its History, Principles, and Transactions to January 1, 1849* (Oneida Reserve, N.Y.: Leonard and Co., 1849). After the first year the association consisted of twenty-nine men, twenty-nine women, and twenty-nine children (twenty-three between the ages of one and ten; fifteen between ten and twenty years; eighteen between twenty and thirty years; twenty-one between thirty and forty years; and ten between forty and fifty years of age).

4   Oneida Community, *Bible Communism: A Compilation from the Annual Reports and other Publications of the Oneida Association and its Branches; Presenting, in Connection with their History, a Summary View of their Religious and Social Theories* (1853; reprint, New York: AMS Press, 1973), p. 22, quoted in Carden, *Oneida*, p. 26.

5   "Scraps and Talks," *Circular*, 2 December 1868; cited in Carol Weisbrod, *The Boundaries of Utopia* (New York: Pantheon Books, 1980), p. 93.

6   T. L. P., "Democracy as Finality," *Circular*, 17 October 1861, pp. 146–47.

7   Ibid., p. 10.

8   John H. Noyes, "Democratic Theocracy."

9   See also Carden, *Oneida*, p. 88.

10   *Circular*, 10 February 1859; quoted in Robertson, *Oneida Community: An Autobiography*, p. 46.

11 Oneida Community, *Handbook and Mutual Criticism* (1871), p. 18.

12 Oneida Community, *Handbook and Mutual Criticism* (1876), pp. 22–23; see also pp. 29–43.

13 Ibid., p. 80.

14 Ibid., pp. 70–71.

15 Weber, *From Max Weber*, pp. 347–48.

16 Noyes criticized conventional marriage arrangements on many occasions. These issues have been distilled in Oneida Community, *Bible Communism*, p. 37. DeMaria (*Communal Love at Oneida*) has combed all Noyes's and the Oneida Community's writings, extracting their ideas on marriage, sex, and love, and should be referred to by anyone interested in an exhaustive account.

17 Oneida Community, *Handbook and Mutual Criticism* (1871), pp. 56–57.

18 Oneida Community, *Bible Communism*, pp. 29–30.

19 Ibid., p. 57.

20 See John H. Noyes, "Home-Talk" on ascending and descending fellowship, in Barron and Miller, *Home-Talks*, pp. 203–9; and DeMaria, *Communal Love at Oneida*, pp. 147–55.

21 Oneida Community, *Bible Communism*, pp. 45–47. The economic metaphors are in the original and are not unusual for the time. See Barker-Benfield, "Spermatic Economy," pp. 45–75.

22 John H. Noyes, *Male Continence* (Oneida: Office of the Oneida Circular, 1872), p. 12.

23 Ibid., pp. 10–17.

24 Carden, *Oneida*, p. 41; Oneida Community, *Handbook and Mutual Criticism* (1871), p. 28, for census figures.

25 Robertson, *Oneida Community: Autobiography*, pp. 337–38.

26 Oneida Community, *Bible Communism*, p. 20.

27 DeMaria, *Communal Love at Oneida*, pp. 162–63.

28 Oneida Community, *Handbook and Mutual Criticism* (1871), p. 27.

29 *Circular*, 15 February 1869, p. 378; cited in DeMaria, *Communal Love at Oneida*, p. 181.

30 P. Noyes, *My Father's House*, p. 65.

31 Ibid., p. 47.

32 Ibid., p. 109.

33 See Weisbrod, *Boundaries of Utopia*, for a fascinating discussion of how nineteenth-century utopian communities fared in the courts and how contract law was used in their protection.

34 Quoted in Robertson, *Oneida Community: The Breakup*, p. 10.

35 Charles Nordhoff, *The Communistic Societies of the United States, from Personal Observation* (1865; reprint, New York: Dover Publications, 1966), p. 266.

36 A. W. C[arr], "Community Journal" [Oneida, N.Y.], covers the period 1 January 1863–16 September 1864, p. 51.

37 See Noyes, *History of American Socialisms*, p. 643.

38 Oneida Community, *Record*, 23 May 1864. This was an internal record of daily community events kept from 1 January 1863 to 15 September 1864; and Parker, *A Yankee Saint*, p. 289.

39 "A Business Glance," *Circular*, 26 September 1854, p. 220; quoted in Robert S. Fogarty, "Oneida: A Utopian Search," p. 220.

40 Carden, *Oneida*, p. 48.

41 Parker, *A Yankee Saint*, p. 230.

42 *Circular*, 1870, p. 5; cited in Parker, *A Yankee Saint*, pp. 254–55.

43 C[arr], "Community Journal," 17 July 1863, p. 51.

8   The Breakup of the Oneida Community

1 See Whitworth, *God's Blueprint*, pp. 215–16.

2 *Perfectionist*, November 1843, p. 73; quoted in Whitworth, *God's Blueprint*, p. 153.

3 Robertson, *Oneida Community: The Breakup*, pp. 56–57.

4 Comstock had sponsored a state law forbidding publication of immoral works, and in 1873 persuaded Congress to pass a federal antiobscenity bill that, among other things, forbade the dissemination of all literature dealing with birth control. Both measures put a serious damper on community publications because they could no longer publicly discuss Oneida's familial and sexual practices.

5 Whitworth, *God's Blueprint*, pp. 217–18.

6 Joseph Bensman and Michael Givant, "Charisma and Modernity: The Use and Abuse of a Concept," *Social Research* 42 (Winter 1975): 612.

7 *Circular*, 4 April 1870, p. 21.

8 See Kingsley Davis, *Human Society* (New York: Macmillan Co., 1948), pp. 175–94.

9 From the private unpublished journal of Francis Wayland-Smith, quoted by Robertson, *Oneida Community: The Breakup*, pp. 91–92.

10 This account of the debate over stirpiculture and the end of complex marriage is taken from Robertson, *Oneida Community: The Breakup*, pp. 144–46.

11 The full text of Noyes's letter appears in ibid., pp. 153–55.

12 John Humphrey Noyes, "Circumscribed Marriage," reprinted in ibid., pp. 190–96.

13 John Humphrey Noyes, *History of American Socialisms*, p. 19.

14 The following is taken from Robertson, *Oneida Community: The Breakup*, pp. 34–37.

15   From an unpublished George W. Noyes manuscript, quoted in Robertson, *Oneida Community: The Breakup*, p. 45.

16   Theodore Noyes had Towner and Hinds in mind. Rumor had them and their followers contemplating secession to form a free-love community. The full texts of the T. Noyes, Wayland-Smith, and Burnham letters are found in Robertson, *Oneida Community: The Breakup*, pp. 201–8.

17   The details of the reorganization period to 1881 are found in ibid., pp. 280–316. Carden, *Oneida*, takes the history into the twentieth century.

18   P. Noyes, *My Father's House*, pp. 192–93.

Index

Mandelker, Ira L., 1952–
Religion, society, and utopia in nineteenth-century
America.
Includes bibliographical references and index.
1. Oneida Community—History—19th century. 2. Collective
settlements—United States—Case studies. I. Title.
HX656.05M36   1984   335'.9747'64   84-47
ISBN 0–87023–436–6